21 DAYS
TO A SATISFIED LIFE

ENCOURAGING WORDS FOR
FABULOUS DAYS

B...

D1373923

HARRISON HOUSE
TULSA, OK

12 11 10 09   10 9 8 7 6 5 4 3 2 1

21 Days to a Satisfied Life—Encouraging Words for Fabulous Days
ISBN 13: 978-1-57794-966-4
ISBN 10: 1-57794-966-8
Copyright © 2009 by Beth Ann Jones
2500 Vincent Dr.
Portage, MI 49024
www.bethjones.org

Published by Harrison House Publishers
P.O. Box 35035
Tulsa, Oklahoma 74153
www.harrisonhouse.com

Contents

Introduction

My soul shall be satisfied.

Psalm 63:5

Satisfaction in life seems to be elusive for so many of us. I know some of the nicest women, wives, and moms. They would do anything for you. They are great moms, school volunteers, businesspeople, friendly, and just plain nice. Yet a number of them have a void in their hearts that is not filled and they live in fear, anxiety, anger, jealousy, worry about their children, and the fear of death. It's sad to see them continually putting the square peg in the round hole of their hearts. They are "almost" fulfilled, "nearly" satisfied, but not genuinely. Blaise Pascal, the seventeenth century French mathematician and physicist, explained, "There is a God-shaped vacuum in the heart of every person and it can never be filled by any created thing. It can only be filled by God, made known through Jesus Christ."

It's true. Unfortunately, a lot of people are trying unsuccessfully to fill that void with substitutes. Substitutes just don't cut it. We need something real. If that's how you feel, *21 Days to a Satisfied Life* can help you on your way to fulfilling your dream of a satisfied life. It has been written for women, wives, and moms of all ages, stages, and seasons who are looking for the real thing.

A certain woman in the Bible found the real thing in life. She had a high "get it" factor. Her name? The Proverbs 31 Woman. She got it. She was the ideal Christian gal. She had it together. She loved God. She was a great wife, her kids loved her, she was successful in business enterprises and ministry, she was a good friend, she dressed to the nines, she was fun, wise, hip, and had it going on. The best thing about her was that everything about her stemmed from her walk with God—she found the satisfied life through her relationship with the Lord. In this book you will see that for yourself as we look at this modern, balanced, Christian woman and the secrets of Proverbs 31. We are going to get to know this gal and believe God that her traits will rub off on us!

One thing you'll find is that she spoke with wisdom and kindness. (v. 26.) Taking time to meditate on and memorize God's Word is invaluable; hiding His Word in our hearts will fill us with His wisdom and love, strengthen us for the present, and arm us for the future. So at the end of each entry you'll find a verse to memorize and chew (meditate) on. I encourage you to write them on index cards and carry them with you. Post them in your bathroom, dashboard, desk, locker, or other convenient places, and soon you'll find them taking root in your heart. Before long, your soul will thirst for God and long for Him like you were "in a dry and thirsty land, where there no water is" (Ps. 63:1). The Hebrew word that refers to total satisfaction and water comes from a root word meaning "to be... saturated...drink one's fill... abundantly satisfy."[1] As you read this book, you'll find that God is the only One who can truly satisfy our "longing [thirsty] soul" (Ps. 107:9).

Whether you are a teen, a Gen-X'er, a Buster, a Boomer, a Golden Gen, or a Geezer, I believe this book will help lead you to a satisfied life in Jesus Christ. So turn your "expectation" on and as you read, trust God to speak to your heart.

Day 1

Cultivate Inner Beauty

**The fear of the LORD leads to life, and he
who has it will abide in satisfaction.**
Proverbs 19:23 NKJV

Ever met a really pretty, ugly girl? Externally, she's
okay, maybe average looking, but internally she's absolutely stunning? How about the ugly, pretty girl? She is
show-stopping, head-turning gorgeous; but internally
she is sad, unfulfilled, self-absorbed, bitter, gossipy,
ego-driven, competitive, two-faced, and phony-baloney.
Ever met her? Are you that girl?

Image. Style. Beauty. Who's got it? Who doesn't?
Teenage girls are fixated on it. Anorexia, bulimia, and
suicide prove that. Moms, wives, and women of all ages
are spending time and lots of money on insta-beauty.
I am all for doing the best we can with what we have
to work with, but what is real beauty? The Bible gives
us the bottom line: "What matters is not your outer
appearance—the styling of your hair, the jewelry you
wear, the cut of your clothes—but your inner disposition. Cultivate inner beauty, the gentle, gracious kind
that God delights in" (1 Peter 3:3–4 MSG).

Cultivate inner beauty? I was hoping for something easier, weren't you? I love a girls' shopping day or an occasional day of pampering. And, although I grew up as a tomboy, I have my share of mid-life, high mainte-nance issues: fill it, color it, wax it, whiten it, exfoliate it, soak it...I'm sure you know the drill. We try to have outer beauty on our terms. The only problem is that there are not enough salons, salts, sugars, lotions, crèmes, botox injections, aroma oils, spas, stylists, or artists on the planet to make us beautiful inside.

The Proverbs 31 Woman had to know about real beauty and real life in God. Her beauty came from within because the best thing about her was that every-thing beautiful about her life stemmed from her walk with God: "Charm and grace are deceptive, and beauty is vain [because it is not lasting], but a woman who reverently and worshipfully fears the Lord, she shall be praised!" (Prov. 31:30 AMP).

It's interesting that in the entire Proverbs 31 passage, this is the only verse that talks about this woman's rela-tionship with the Lord. As you look at that chapter, it is obvious that her walk with God splashes over beau-tifully into every other area of her life. Cultivating a relationship with God (the ultimate beauty essential!) means talking with Him regularly, reading His Word, and getting to know Him. It creates peace of mind and heart, feeling loved and accepted, fulfilled, joyful, content, and satisfied. Lack of this relationship creates an internal aching void inside of us. Many people try to fill that void with other things from addictions to money, parties, status, you name it—yet come up empty and never satisfied. When we are united to and enjoy a friendship with God, we can live the satisfying life He intended. Our hearts don't want to displease or disobey Him, but rather we want to know Him, walk with Him, and please Him.

If we try to fix all our internal issues using external remedies, we're wasting precious time. Worry, depression, fear, guilt, stress, anger, bitterness, and jealousy create wrinkles, sad eyes, and severe facial expressions that even the best makeup can't fix! The only way to get "the glow" is to give our attention to "inner remedies." So, for real beauty, here are five essentials every girl needs in her "cosmetic bag."

→ Foundation ∞ A real, genuine relationship with the Lord will give you a great foundational canvas to build on.

→ Blush ∞ Get rid of the stuff that makes you blush! Purify your mind and heart using this easy test: if it would make your grandma blush, give it a flush!

→ Eye Shadow ∞ Fix your eyes on the needs of others; look for ways to be a blessing and root them on.

→ Lipstick ∞ Pray a lot and watch the words that come out of your mouth, nothing critical, nothing bitter.

➺ Cover Up ∞ Extend forgiveness to others frequently. Love covers.

Have you noticed that when we give the "inner man" the attention it deserves it helps to make the outer appearance more beautiful? There's a sparkle in the eyes. There's an easy smile. There's a glow of satisfaction on the face. Congruence in the inner man makes the beautiful, ugly girl—a Pretty Woman!

Scripture to Chew On

Charm and grace are deceptive, and beauty is vain [because it is not lasting], but a woman who reverently and worshipfully fears the Lord, she shall be praised!
Proverbs 31:30 AMP

Booster Shot For Your Satisfied Life

Our hearts are filled with all kinds of things that are not acceptable to God when we are not a Christian. Even after we become a Christian, our hearts can get clogged up at times with things that can hinder our walk with the Lord. What kinds of things are going on inside your heart? What's coming out of your heart? Have you been using external remedies to fix internal issues? Today, be sure to give yourself an inner beauty treatment using the five things from your "cosmetic bag."

Day 2

Love and Value Yourself

> What is the price of five sparrows—two copper coins? Yet God does not forget a single one of them. And the very hairs on your head are all numbered. So don't be afraid; you are more valuable to God than a whole flock of sparrows.
>
> *Luke 12:6,7 NLT*

What's the most expensive thing you own? How do you treat it? Do you let every Tom, Dick, and Harry insult it, criticize it, and beat it up? Do you give yourself the same respect you give your expensive trinkets? Don't settle for anything less. It's necessary for the satisfaction and success of your life to have a healthy self-worth. You don't have to be a narcissist. But the reality is that you can't truly value and love others until you love and value yourself.

I meet too many women with a low self-worth, women who don't feel good about themselves. They live so far below their potential, it's pitiful. A lot of high school, college, and single girls, and even some married gals cheapen themselves by giving their hearts or bodies to some sweet-talking man (other than their husband) for nothing more than a drink or a movie. They put up with such abuse and disrespect, it's heartbreaking (they shouldn't put up with that even if it's their husband). They are sad, mad, and sometimes bad.

The experts say that nearly 90 percent of the population has a low self-image. They don't realize how valuable they are. In various ways, we've all been there. Are you there right now? Maybe you don't know your value.

You are an expensive girl and it's time you start acting like it. You are more valuable than you realize. You need to see yourself the way your Creator does. God's view of you is found in a verse about the Proverbs 31 Woman: "A worthy woman who can find? For her price is far above rubies" (v. 10 ASV). Have you priced a ruby lately? I have. According to a local jeweler, you could spend as much as $25,000 for a one carat ruby! Well, your value is far above rubies—that's rubies, *plural*. You are not equated with some sliver of a cubic zirconia—no, your value is far above rubies. So, woman…how much are you worth?

Proverbs 31:10 reminds us of our value in God's eyes—we are already highly valued as His daughters. When we were sinners, God loved and valued us enough to send His Son Jesus to our rescue. (John 3:16.) Two thousand years ago, God in the flesh came to Earth and walked on the planet He created. He chose to die on a cross in order to shed His spotless blood for the forgiveness of our sins. He wanted to be our substitute in paying the penalty of death that sin demanded, so that we wouldn't have to pay that penalty by being separated from the Father in a place called hell. After God's justice was served, He raised Jesus from the dead and now Jesus is at the right hand of God and is also interceding for us.[1] (Rom. 8:34.)

In Mel Gibson's movie *The Passion of The Christ*, the price God paid for us was all so vivid and brutal. "Right before your very eyes—Jesus Christ (the Messiah) was openly and graphically set forth and portrayed as crucified" (Galatians 3:1 AMP). Why? Jesus paid the highest price to purchase us, and it's important that we rest in the fact that He already values us highly.

You are so valuable to God that He made you one-of-a-kind! You don't have to be like everyone else. You don't have to go along with the crowd. You have not been made like anyone else. You are an original! Be encouraged today...

> You are not a mistake.
> You are a special person.
> You are gifted.
> You are highly favored.
> You are more intelligent than you realize.
> You are full of creative potential.
> You are extremely good looking.
> You are marvelous.

You are accepted.

You are created in God's image.

You are loved.

Maybe you need to be reminded of the old saying, "God don't make no junk." Today, throw caution to the wind and just be the one-of-a-kind, original, valuable person God has created you to be. You are God's jewel and highly valued—don't you forget it. Respect and value yourself. Recognize your worth and be willing to esteem your value. Let's not insult God by thinking less of ourselves than He does.

Scripture to Chew On

Thank you for making me so wonderfully complex! Your workmanship is marvelous—and how well I know it.

Psalm 139:14 NLT

Booster Shot For Your Satisfied Life

God thinks you're worth more than rubies as He's paid quite a price for you. Isn't it nice to know that He loves, accepts, and cares about you? He has made you to be one-of-a-kind with unique and complex traits. Do you recognize any of them? How can you best use them in your everyday life?

Day 3

Dive In to the World's Bestseller

I will meditate on Your precepts, and contemplate Your ways. I will delight myself in Your statutes; I will not forget Your word.

Psalm 119:15,16 NKJV

I love God's Word. He has revealed Himself, changed, and upgraded every area of my life as I have simply read, believed, and obeyed the Bible. But it wasn't always that way. Like many people, I had never even considered reading the Bible for myself, much less studying it. The Bible was for priests, theologians, and monks. It was not relevant to my life. It was a dusty old book in our basement.

One day, when I was 14 years old, I just got a strong desire to read the Bible. I started with Genesis, and within the first few chapters I fell asleep. That was the end of my Bible reading until I was a 19-year-old college freshman. My roommate began to share with me what the Bible said about God, about life, and about me, so I started reading the Bible again and was shocked at the "living" quality of God's Word. It wasn't like any other book I'd read. This wasn't like reading a president's biography or the dull Western Civilization textbooks from my class. It was as if God Himself was explaining the contents to me.

Isn't it great that the Bible is interactive—not just historic or static? God's Word is living and active and able to effectually work within us to affect change and impart the miraculous. The Bible is a supernatural book. It took 1,500 years to write the Bible and it was written by forty different people who had different careers—fisherman, farmers, doctors, kings, and preachers. Some of them were even from different generations. Not only that but it was written in three different languages—Hebrew, Aramaic, and Greek. Yet the Bible has one central theme—Jesus Christ is the star of every part of Scripture. It is obvious that there was really One Supreme Author—God, the Holy Spirit, was in charge of the writing.

The Bible is the most amazing book ever. It has been banned, burned, and blasted, but it lives on and continues to be the world's bestselling book. As a new believer and a sophomore in college, my Bible study leader simply exhorted me to read the Bible and let the Word of Christ dwell richly inside of me. It was the best advice ever! As I continued to read it, something was happening in my heart. I was challenged. I was encouraged. I was comforted. The Living God was speaking through His Living Word. I stayed up late to read the Bible. I pondered it during the day. There was plenty I didn't understand, but I received strength, energy, and wisdom just by reading it, and ultimately the Holy Spirit drew me to Jesus. As I read my Bible, Jesus walked off the pages and came to live in my heart. Jesus isn't just alive in heaven, He is alive to me. I've come to know Him intimately through friendship with Him in His Word. The result was that I began to develop an insatiable appetite for God and His Word and a passionate desire to share His Word with others.

When you read your Bible, it's like eating spiritual food for your spirit to grow strong, just like you eat food every day for your body to grow strong. The Bible will give you spiritual food, strength, light, power, and direction; it will teach you everything you need to know about how to walk in God's blessings in this life. It's no wonder Satan fights so hard to distract you and keep you from reading it! If you will read your Bible every day, God will show you many things about His love and all that He has planned for your life.

Perhaps you are facing a decision in a relationship or in your job or in changing careers or in purchasing a home or in a call to ministry, or in some other situation, but you just aren't sure what to do. Don't try to figure it out and don't just go with logic and reason; get into the Word and trust God to give you a word to light up your path. God will speak to you through His Word and He will give you the precise direction you need. He will let you know what choice to make and give you the grace you need to follow through. The anointed Word of God has the power to effectually work within a person giving faith, light, direction, freedom, healing, joy, peace, deliverance, wisdom, revelation, hope, instruction, correction, salvation, growth, maturity, and fruit. Siding with God's Word is always a safe guide!

Remember how the Proverbs 31 Woman reverentially feared the Lord? (v. 30.) If we do likewise the way she did, we will love God's Word. We will feed on, believe in, and be obedient to do His Word. The Lord has our best interest in mind, so we can rest in the knowledge that following His Word is the wise and safe thing to do. And when we live a life worthy of the Lord and fully pleasing to Him, we qualify for His amazing blessings! (See Deut. 6:2–15; Prov. 31.)

Scripture to Chew On

**Man shall not live by bread alone, but by
every word that proceeds from the mouth
of God.**

Matthew 4:4 NKJV

Booster Shot For Your Satisfied Life

Before you begin to read the Bible: *pray*—ask God,
by the Holy Spirit, to customize the Scriptures for you
personally; *expect*—turn your "expectation" on and trust
God to speak to your heart; *dive*—grab your Bible, pen,
and favorite beverage, and dive in! If your life has been a
series of missteps and self-made disappointments, spend
extra time reading your Bible and allow the Lord to lead
you into a good place as He gives you a lamp for your
feet and a light for your path. (Ps. 119:105.)

Day 4

Frame Your World with
Your Words

> **By faith we understand that the worlds were framed by the word of God, so that the things which are seen were not made of things which are visible.**
>
> *Hebrews 11:3 NKJV*

If you've ever built a house or been involved with a construction project, you know how important the frame is. Once the foundation is poured, it's critical that the framing—all the beams, posts and studs—goes up plumb or it will mess up the whole building. What would curtains look like on windows hung on a wall framed at 45 degrees? How would you close a door that was set on a frame missing its header or footer? Can you imagine how funky a house or building would look with pieces of frame sticking out from a wall or ceiling at random places? Talk about no satisfaction! A proper frame is imperative. A building without a strong, balanced, well-built frame will be a structural disaster.

The same thing is true in our own lives. When our lives are built on the foundation of Jesus Christ, it's important to pay attention to the "framing" that goes up on that foundation. We have the ability to frame our world with words...God's words. The Bible tells us that in the same way God framed the world with His words and He called things that "be not as though they were" (Rom. 4:17), so too, we can frame our world (our relationship with the Lord, our emotional, mental, physical health and strength, our relationships, marriage, families, finances, and so on) by speaking God's Word.

Think about the way God made the world. He spoke words and framed the seen world with things that are not seen. God's words brought things which are not visible into the visible realm. This is God's principle of faith: "God, who gives life to the dead and calls those things which do not exist as though they did" (v. 17 NKJV). This is the power of God's spoken Word.

How's your world being framed? Are things hanging well for you? Are windows and doors opening for you? Do you have a strong, godly structure upon which to build the rest of your life? Is your life plumb and congruent with God's best? I believe the Proverbs 31 Woman framed her world with her words, as verse 26 says, "She opens her mouth with wisdom, and on her tongue is the law of kindness [or the Gospel[1]]" (NKJV). If you haven't been, are you willing to begin framing your world with God's Word? Are you ready to call things that do not exist as though they did?

God's Son Jesus told us one way of doing that is by praying that God's kingdom would come and His will would be done on earth as it is in heaven. (Matt. 6:10.) God in heaven has a will that includes a host of things—from the destiny of nations to His detailed purposes for each individual. When we get into the Word to hear from Him, we discover what His will in heaven is and we can then pray an effective prayer that gets it done on earth.

God made it simple. Prayer starts with God. He has a will. If we spend time seeking Him and reading His Word, we discover His will. When we pray according to His will, He hears us and answers. If we want to live the supernatural, victorious, satisfying Christian life He planned for us, we must line up our mouths with His Word. When we discover what the Word says about who we are in Christ and what belongs to us in Christ, we must choose to say those things. Over time, those words can frame our lives.

In order to use words effectively, we must know the Word. The Bible is loaded with exhortations about the words we speak and their power to frame our lives. For instance,

- *We eat the fruit of our words* (Prov. 18:20–21 NKJV)
- *We bring forth things with words* (Matt. 12:34-37 NKJV)
- *We can turn our whole body around with words* (James 3:3–5 NKJV)
- *We move mountains with words* (Mark 11:23 NKJV)

Why not make a big change? Start eliminating idle and inoperative words, and, instead, frame your world by only saying what God says about your life—spirit, soul, and body. If you'll become a student of the Word and spend time filling your heart with the knowledge of the "it is written," you won't be an easy target for the enemy, and you'll have the weapons you need to stand strong and build the kind of satisfying life God wants for you!

Scripture to Chew On

They…continued to speak God's Word with fearless confidence.

Acts 4:31 MSG

Booster Shot For Your Satisfied Life

The Word of God is powerful. When we speak it, God's power is dispensed to us in a customized and dynamic way to meet our needs. Along with Scripture, something else that's powerful is to declare and decree Jesus' name over our lives. His name has all power in heaven and earth. And the big bonus? He has given us the authority to use His name. He has deputized us with the "power of attorney" to pray, say, decree, declare, bind, loose, and operate in the authority that His name carries as we walk with Him in the light of His Word. You may be "behind the curve" in framing your world by speaking the Word and Jesus' name, but you can change. Start today to say the kinds of words that will frame your life the way God intends.

Day 5

Operate By the Spirit
of Generosity

Generous people plan to do what is generous, and they stand firm in their generosity.

Isaiah 32:8 NLT

The Proverbs 31 Woman had an amazing MO. She was not only an astute businessperson and industrious worker, she had a spirit of generosity. (See v. 20.) She employed God's laws of sowing and reaping in her life and reaped some great results. We can do the same! This law of seedtime and harvest is a spiritual law. We do reap what we sow—naturally, spiritually, financially, relationally, and so on. As Christians, our MO is to be generous. Of course, this is the exact opposite of how the world thinks.

Earthly treasures are not secure nowadays. Jesus told us this fact almost 2,000 years ago (Matt. 6:19–21), and we've had an "up-close and personal" look at this truth in the problems many people have experienced in their retirement accounts, 401(k)s, earnings, and equity. In times of instability and fear due to economic conditions, if you're not a believer and you don't have the Lord or believe the Word, you have no hope. The good news is God has a better way, and those who have followed His principles have discovered that His economic and banking plan is better than the world's system.

If you're struggling financially, I encourage you to jump into God's economy. His economy is based on a completely different paradigm—giving! The world says to get all you can and keep all you get. Jesus said to give all you can and it will be given back to you good measure, pressed down, shaken together, and running over. (Luke 6:38.) Remember, most things that relate to the Lord are the exact opposite of the world. So if you want to be great in God's kingdom, you don't push and shove and claw your way to the top; you become a servant of all. You humble yourself and God will exalt you. And, if you want to be blessed in life and have abundance, you don't hoard it up and be greedy, you do the exact opposite. You operate by the spirit of generosity and become a giver in all the different areas of your life.

Jesus told us, "Do not lay up for yourselves treasures on earth, where moth and rust destroy and where thieves break in and steal; but lay up for yourselves treasures in heaven, where neither moth nor rust destroys and where thieves do not break in and steal. For where your treasure is, there your heart will be also" (Matt. 6:19–21 NKJV). Many of us have read this passage and thought this meant that we should love heaven more than earth. We've thought it meant that as we give to God's kingdom we should be content knowing that we won't see those treasures again until we get to heaven—when God rewards us. That may be so, but there is another important aspect of this passage.

When we seek God's kingdom first (by spending time alone with Him, praying, and reading His Word daily), and when we act that out by laying up our treasures in heaven—through tithes, offerings, and alms—we are putting our money where our heart is; we are literally laying up treasures for ourselves in a safe place. Those treasures aren't just for when we get to heaven—they are for the here and now, too. We can access and make withdrawals on this heavenly account now, by faith, and God makes sure we can access them now. In fact, God has literally promised that He'll open the windows of heaven and pour out those treasures we have stored up in such a way that there won't be room enough to receive it. (Mal. 3:10.) I don't know how He does it, but He finds ways to protect and multiply the financial seeds we sow and supernaturally gets those treasures circulated back into our lives while we are on earth!

Living by a spirit of generosity is not just about money. We can carry a spirit of generosity in our worship, our prayer life, our thanks, words, actions, and relationships, in service in church, ministry, and toward people, by being kind and gracious and sharing the joy of the Lord with others. Generosity is a force and when that force comes out of us, we're able to live in a higher place. At a restaurant, when the menu promises a generous portion, you are expecting it to be bigger than normal, better than average. Or when you get an outfit and the tag on it says generous sizes, you expect it to be bigger. As Christians, we ought to be such people that this generosity thing comes out of us and it's just not normal, it's not like the average. People know what to expect in the norm, or the average response. If you're a Christian and this force of generosity comes out of you, it's above average, it's supernatural. Generous people stand out!

What must generous people look like to others now in these "last days" when the love of many has grown cold, as Jesus said, and people have become "lovers of themselves and lovers of their money" as the apostle Paul stated? (Matt. 24:12 NKJV; 2 Tim. 3:2 NKJV.) Many exhibit the opposite of generosity; they're self-absorbed. But God's generosity is off the charts!

God is the One who is the originator of generosity. Everything after His original model is the copy, it's the imitation, and we're supposed to mimic and copy Him! God is generous, kind, and overflowing towards us. He's a giver, not a withholder; He gives good things in abundance; He's not cheap, chintzy, or stingy. And He's looking for copycats! He wants us to imitate Him: to be generous, be givers, give good things, and give in abundance. So be generous on purpose. The force of generosity coming out of us repels the things coming against us. Instead of the forces of this world coming against us and things like self-pity, depression, and anxieties weighing us down until we feel like we're under it, if we'll purpose to be generous people, by generosity we shall stand (arise, rise up), succeed, and be abundantly blessed!

Scripture to Chew On

The generous soul will be made rich, and he who waters will also be watered himself.
Proverbs 11:25 NKJV

Booster Shot For Your Satisfied Life

Kids love to jump off diving boards into swimming pools. They want to do a cannonball and see who can make the biggest splash. Sometimes kids do a pencil dive, jumping off the board and going straight into the water without making any splash. Some Christians are cannonball Christians. The force of generosity coming out of us can splash people. The bigger the splash, the more people are touched by our generosity. Other Christians are pencil Christians and make no splash at all. How big is your splash?

Day 6

Be "Under the Influence"

**These are not drunk, as you suppose…
but this is what was spoken by the prophet
Joel…that I will pour out of My Spirit on
all flesh.**

Acts 2:15–17 NKJV

Getting wasted. Drunk. Plastered. Totaled. Trashed. Stoned. TGIF. It all speaks to the cultural epidemic of our age…excessive drinking.

In spite of all the arguments and realities against drinking that are supposed to tell partiers why to quit drinking, I think we are still missing the point. People drink for a reason. They want to feel good! They are tired of the rat race, emptiness, disappointments, challenges, and pace of life and they want to get "under the influence" of something else. They want to laugh. They want to be uninhibited. They want to be numb. They want to be empowered. Alcohol has a way of intoxicating people to the bummers of life.

The only problem is that alcohol is the counterfeit. Millions of people have been duped into using a counterfeit for relief, because they've never tasted the real. There is a real intoxicant—the real McCoy—and it's not alcohol. The real way to be "under the influence" is to tap into the living God.

It's true. God never intended for us to go through life sober. He knows life is tough; that's why He's provided the ultimate intoxicant. The Bible tells us about it in Ephesians 5:18: "Don't be drunk with wine… but be filled with the Spirit" (NKJV). That's the real deal.

I've been wasted with the best of 'em. I know what it's like to be plastered, giddy, and hung over with the room spinning. Been there, done it. When I finally realized that the temporary fix alcohol brought was just a substitute for the real deal, everything changed for me. When I invited Jesus into my life and got filled with the Holy Spirit, I found a continual hookup to God's finest intoxicant. Being filled and living under the influence of the Spirit opens up a whole new world!

Spirit-filled believers notice that the Word comes alive in a fresh way; they seem to receive more and more light and revelation as they study God's Word. They experience a new boldness and power in their witness for Christ. The presence of God in their hearts and their freedom in praise and worship takes on a whole new dimension. Being filled with the Spirit is really the "gateway" to the realm of the Spirit. It's the escape route from "Christianity as usual."

Does something inside of you believe "there is more" for you as a believer, despite what you've been told? How well do you know the Holy Spirit?

The Holy Spirit is a very real person. He is the third person of the Godhead or Trinity. The Trinity is made up of the Father, Son, and Holy Spirit. The Holy Spirit is a person, not an "it" or an impersonal "force." We are supposed to know the Holy Spirit—be led by Him, commune with Him, listen to Him, find comfort in Him, guidance, revelation, help, strength, intercession with Him, and power through Him.

The Bible teaches us that the Holy Spirit wants to do a mighty work in and through our lives, yet sometimes the subject of being filled with the Holy Spirit is confusing and controversial.

In John 7:37–39, Jesus is telling believers that when they are filled with the Spirit they will receive rivers of living water that will flow up from their spirit and out to refresh others. This fits perfectly with the purpose of being Spirit-filled—that is, to be a witness for Jesus. See, when we are "born of" the Spirit (or born again), God puts a well inside of us—a well of living water; a well of salvation. We can draw water from that well at any time to find refreshing in Christ. When we are "filled with" the Spirit (or Spirit-filled), God puts rivers inside of us—rivers of living water that flow out from us. We can yield to the Spirit and those rivers will flow out of us to touch others with God's love and power.

Need a supernatural intoxicating jolt today? Need God's resurrection power to fill every cell, fiber, bone, nerve, tissue, muscle, organ and system of your body? Need your youth to be renewed like the eagle's?

Maybe you feel like you need a small army to help you function, survive, and thrive in life. Someone to wrap you in their arms and comfort you while at the same time give you intensive counseling, extra help, and the power of their supernatural prayers. Or perhaps you need someone to stand up for you and be your defense attorney while at the same time imparting inner strength into the core of your being. And…just in case you start to fade, they are there "on standby" to jump into action in any one of these capacities. We have such an army—the Greater One, the Holy Spirit! (See John 14:16 AMP.)

Yes, there are many benefits of being filled with the Spirit. The problem is we live in a society that has largely rejected God and all He offers and has settled for the substitutes, counterfeits, and fakes. We've been duped. The result is a party culture that is unhappy, depressed, anxious, angry, obsessive, compulsive, co-dependent, lost, and dissatisfied. The kicker is that a lot of these people are mad at God for all of it! I hope you're not one of those.

If you're tired of the phony, find some people who know how to tap into God and take a drink of His stuff. The more you drink, the better life is. Why not ask for the Holy Spirit's power and influence in your life today?

You can be loaded—full of peace, joy, and laughter in the midst of life's challenges—with no hangovers! Cheers.

Scripture to Chew On

Not by might, nor by power, but by my spirit, saith the LORD of hosts.

Zechariah 4:6

Booster Shot For Your Satisfied Life

The Proverbs 31 Woman is led by the Spirit. If you are a believer, then you are ready to receive the Holy Spirit in His fullness by simply asking the Father to fill you with the Spirit and yielding to the Holy Spirit. One benefit is that as a child of God, His Spirit is supposed to be leading you. Often the Holy Spirit will let you know things about your children, your spouse, and your own life before they happen. If you stay sensitive to God in prayer and in seeking Him and listening to the Holy Spirit, He will often tip you off or He will supernaturally show or impress upon you things you otherwise would not know. Can you think of a time when the Holy Spirit impressed something upon you like this? If you need Him to do that for you now, what can you do to hear from Him?

Day 7

Change Your Clothes

As God's chosen people, holy and dearly loved, clothe yourselves with compassion, kindness, humility, gentleness and patience. Bear with each other and forgive whatever grievances you may have against one another. Forgive as the Lord forgave you. And over all these virtues put on love, which binds them all together in perfect unity.

Colossians 3:12–14 NIV

If you've watched any of the fashion TV shows, you know those clothing experts can be brutal! They take one look at someone's style and cut them to shreds. These fashionistas really do have an eye for style and in the end, they make the dowdiest, mismatched person look amazing.

God is the Eternal Fashionista. He knows what attitudes and behaviors are best on us. He's not as harsh as some of the TV show hosts, but He does delight in trashing our selfish, proud, mean-spirited, and impatient outfits. He helps us see ourselves in the mirror of His Word so that we can toss out any "fashion statements" that reflect moodiness, discontentedness, resentment, and bitterness.

He knows what not to wear because He paid the highest price to purchase what to wear—for us. The Lord has some very fine threads for us! He wants us to put on the designer garment of compassion for others—feeling their pain enough to be moved to do something about it. He wants us to accessorize our lives with kindness, humility, and patience. He wants us to wear the high style of being even-tempered and willing to bear with others. Most importantly, the Lord wants us dressed to the nines by walking in forgiveness and the all-purpose garment of love.

The Proverbs 31 Woman dresses in designer clothing. Her clothes of tapestry…silk and purple, signify that she puts on the best, finest apparel, suitable to royalty—as the Church is.[1] (Prov. 31:22.) As born-again believers we are to "put on the Lord Jesus Christ" (Rom. 13:14 NKJV). Galatians 3:27 tells us how putting on Christ begins—by being "baptized into Christ," or receiving Him as Savior.[2] To "put on" a person was a Greek phrase often used to mean "to imbibe his principles, to imitate his example, to copy his spirit, to become like him."[3] Sometimes that's easier said than done.

When we are tired, stressed, under pressure, or living by unrealistic expectations, we can find ourselves slipping into comfy, old ungodly attitudes and behaviors. The result is that we become short-fused, snippy, and frustrated. (I know!) The fix is: a quick change! We can run into the dressing room of God's forgiveness and exchange those old duds for the clothing He has provided. He wants us to put off old clothes and put on the new clothes!

Need some help with your spiritual fashion these days? I encourage you to change your clothes and clothe yourself in God's attire. Listen to how the *Message Bible* puts Colossians 3:12–14:

> **So, chosen by God for this new life of love, dress in the wardrobe God picked out for you: compassion, kindness, humility, quiet strength, discipline. Be even-tempered, content with second place, quick to forgive an offense. Forgive as quickly and completely as the Master forgave you. And regardless of what else you put on, wear love. It's your basic, all-purpose garment. Never be without it.**

Notice that on top of all these things, we're to put on love! That means to love more than just the people you like—love your enemies, and pray for them. Over the years, when people have come against Jeff and me or the work of God in and through our church, we made a decision to walk in love. At times, we had to be bold and condemn misinformation or blatant lies by speaking the truth in love and at other times, we said nothing and simply prayed for them.

I distinctly remember one staff prayer meeting when our church was in a battle to obtain an approval to build our new building. We specifically decided to pray for our enemies and you should have heard the staff praying for those who had opposed us! We asked the Lord to bless our opponents and to fill their holidays with His love, great memories, and wonderful times with their families. We chose to pray those prayers by faith because we knew that *love never fails!*

Scripture to Chew On

> [The Proverb 31 Woman's] clothing is of linen, pure and fine, and of purple [such as that of which the clothing of the priests and the hallowed cloths of the temple were made].
>
> *Proverbs 31:22 AMP*

Booster Shot For Your Satisfied Life

Jesus paid a mighty high price by shedding His blood so that we could clothe ourselves in compassion, kindness, humility, quiet strength, discipline, even-temper, contentment, forgiveness, and love. If you have been wearing some old, ugly attitudes, ask Him to forgive you and help you to put off the old clothes and put on those new threads today and every day.

Day 8

Rest In the Fact That
God Is Good

O taste and see that the Lord [our God]
is good! Blessed (happy, fortunate, to be
envied) is the man who trusts and takes
refuge in Him.

Psalm 34:8 AMP

The Lord is good all the time!

It's true and don't let anyone or anything ever
talk you out of that. But, be advised—many voices
will try to convince you otherwise. Often the enemy,
our own thoughts, circumstances, relationships, and
life experiences cause us to question God's goodness.
When we don't fully understand God's big picture,
purposes, timing, kingdom laws, and the hows and
whys of things we face, we sometimes drift around in
the "Yeah, but what about…?" sea of confusion regarding God's goodness.

A lot of people really don't know the God of the
Bible. They have all kinds of ideas about what God is

like based mostly on misinformation, human opinion, personal experiences, or religious traditions—but not always based on a real biblical revelation. Fortunately, God is not mysterious or in hiding. He has openly revealed Himself—His Son Jesus is the visible image of the invisible God!

If you want to know what God is like, look at Jesus. Study His life. Listen to His words. Follow His actions. Jesus perfectly revealed Father God to humanity. When we look at everything Jesus said and did, we get an accurate picture of the character, heart, goodness, and operations of God Almighty.

What did Jesus show us about Father God?

- Jesus always did good things for people. (Acts 10:38.)
- Jesus always showed mercy to the humble. (Matthew 9:13.)
- Jesus healed everyone who came to Him in faith. (Luke 6:19.)
- Jesus did miracles for people. (John 2:11.)
- Jesus taught the Word when people had doubts. (Mark 6:6.)
- Jesus had compassion on people. (Matthew 9:36.)
- Jesus was our substitute in hell; He went there to pay the penalty for our sins so we wouldn't have to. (Psalm 16:10.)

- Jesus had more joy than anyone and showed us it's possible to rejoice always. (Hebrews 1:9.)
- Jesus never sent tragedy, calamity, or sickness to teach someone a lesson. (John 10:10.)
- Jesus always turned impossible situations into possibilities. (Matthew 19:26.)
- Jesus loved sinners. (Luke 7:34.)

Settle this issue once and for all. God is good! He's not schizo-God; He's the same yesterday, today, and forever. (Heb. 13:8.) He is the God who changes not. (Mal. 3:6.) He is good and His intentions toward us are always for our good. We may not always understand everything, but we can rest in the fact that the Lord is good. We can have confidence that as we walk in the light of His Word, He will always bring us through any trial, challenge, or battle we face into a good land. The Bible tells us about God's goodness…

- God is good all the time. (Psalm 52:1 NKJV.)
- He is a good Father. (Luke 12:32.)
- He gives good gifts. (Luke 11:13.)
- He satisfies us with good things. (Psalm 103:5.)
- His good hand is upon us. (Ecclesiastes 2:24.)
- His plans for us are good and not evil. (Jeremiah 29:11 NLT.)
- He wants us to eat the good of the land. (Isaiah 1:19.)

- He goes about doing good things and healing all who are oppressed. (Acts 10:38.)
- He wants us to see good days. (1 Peter 3:10.)
- The Lord is good and His mercy endures forever. (Psalm 107:1.)

Do you believe that God is a good God and that He is for you? Start declaring His goodness to you right now. There may be some things you don't totally understand, but you can settle this issue once and for all by saying out loud: "God, You are good all the time. Your intentions toward me are for my good. You love me and You have good plans for my life. Help me to understand how to cooperate with You and Your Word so that I am walking and living in Your goodness to a greater degree."

I love Psalm 68:19 that says, "Blessed be the Lord, Who daily loads us with benefits" (NKJV). As a new Christian, as I walked in the light of His Word, the Lord helped me to get a hold of this simple revelation—I hope you will grab hold of it too: God is good and He desires to load His kids with benefits!

Scripture to Chew On

I would have lost heart, unless I had
believed that I would see the goodness of
the LORD in the land of the living.

Psalm 27:13 NKJV

Booster Shot For Your Satisfied Life

If you've not been experiencing God's goodness
lately, at least to the degree you believe He desires, Isaiah
1:19 NKJV is a great starting point: "If you are willing
and obedient, you shall eat the good of the land." Apply
this verse immediately. First, take inventory of your life
and ask the Lord if there are any areas where you have
not been willing or obedient to Him. Be brutally honest
with yourself and then make the needed adjustments.
Make a decision to be willing to do whatever He's asking
of you and be obedient to do it. When you do, He has
promised that you can eat the good of the land—you
can have all of the blessings He promises in His Word
to those who obey Him!

Day 9

Put Away the Spear

A heart at peace gives life to the body, but envy rots the bones.

Proverbs 14:30 NIV

When my youngest sister and I were in our early twenties, we visited the home of a very successful surgeon. His house had every bell and whistle; he spared no expense. We muttered under our breath, "Wow, are we jealous or what?" He heard us and said, "Don't ever be jealous of another Christian brother or sister. Be happy for them, knowing you are standing in the same line." At first, I thought, *That's easy for you to say, Mr. Millionaire. Guess it's time for us to leave and drive back to our duplex in our beater Honda CVCC. Mind if we take a handful of peanuts for the road?* But, then I pondered his statement and the light bulb went off for me, *Hey…that's right. We are in the same line—the line of faith and obedience—and in time, if we rejoice with others and stay faithful to God, our turn will come.* Turns out, he was right!

Everyone has to deal with feelings of jealousy and envy at one time or another. If not handled properly, they ruin relationships. They ruin teams. They ruin churches. They ruin lives. So let's take a closer look at these evil twins.

Envy is aware of and resents the advantages enjoyed by others. *Envy* has a burning desire to possess the same blessings. In other words, *envy* wants what others have and until their desires are fulfilled; *envy* resents seeing others blessed.

Jealousy is hostile toward a rival...someone seen as enjoying an advantage or seen as a threat to their position or advantage. In other words, *jealousy* doesn't want others to have any success or advantage over them.

So how do we deal with *jealousy* and *envy* when they come knocking on our door? We can see what to do and what not to do up close in the life of Saul as he freaked out about God's blessings in and on David's life.

As David was returning from a great military success, a slaughter of the Philistines "the women had come out of all the cities of Israel, singing and dancing, to meet King Saul, with tambourines, with joy, and with musical instruments. So the women sang as they danced, and said: 'Saul has slain his thousands, and David his ten thousands.' Then Saul was very angry, and the saying displeased him; and he said, 'They have ascribed to David ten thousands, and to me they have ascribed only thousands. Now what more can he have but the kingdom?'" (1 Sam. 18:6–8 NKJV).

The accolades will do us in if we aren't careful. David was perceived as more successful in war than Saul. Saul had killed thousands and done quite well; it's just that David did better and Saul's envy and jealousy started to sprout.

So, what about us? What if another Christian, co-worker, team member, or staff member starts to get more kudos than we do? What if someone raves about the song someone else sang? What if someone raves about the message someone else preached? What if someone raves about the work that someone else did? If we're not careful, the seeds of envy and jealousy can be easily planted.

When we allow them to take root, envy and jealousy produce bad fruit. Saul's jealous eye got the best of him and the day after David got all those accolades Saul was filled with distress and oppression. (vv. 9–10 NKJV.) Yet look what David did: "David played music with his hand (v. 10)." Don't lose your song if someone else is jealous or envious of you—keep singing! Saul wasn't rejoicing with David's success, but rather, Saul wanted David to go away—and if necessary, Saul was going to take him out. (vv. 10–11 NKJV.) If others don't rejoice with your success, keep singing. If someone is more successful than you are, put away the spear!

The price of envy and jealousy is high: Saul tried to kill David twice with his spear, but David was able to escape Saul's attempts. "Now Saul was afraid of David, because the LORD was with him, but had departed from Saul" (v. 12 NKJV). This is the worst part of the story—Saul's jealousy cost him the anointing, God's presence and favor. The Lord was with David; God picked him to do something unique; God called him—he was going to continue to prosper and succeed. Saul disqualified himself because he did not agree with God. He did not embrace or encourage the one God had called.

Saul promoted David to captain in his army, not to honor David but to appease the people and in hopes that David would be killed in combat. Why didn't his plan work? "David behaved wisely in all his ways, and the LORD was with him. Therefore, when Saul saw that he behaved very wisely, he was afraid of him. But all Israel and Judah loved David" (vv. 14–16 NKJV). Even though Saul was having personal inferiority, depression, anger, jealousy, and envy issues because of David's success, all the other people loved David. God's favor would not leave David, just because Saul's nose got bent out of whack. When you think about it, what did Saul want? Did he want David to fail? Yes! When we are jealous or envious of others, how sick do we have to be to want them to fail so that we can feel secure, superior, or strong in our own identity?

If jealousy and envy have been invading your space, kick them out by proactively walking in God's love and faith, knowing that you are in the same line. The last thing these evil twins want to hear is you being genuinely happy for the success of others, rooting others on, and celebrating their success. So, why not pummel envy and jealousy by blessing, complimenting, being generous toward, encouraging, celebrating, commenting, rejoicing, congratulating, and raving about the very people you have been envious or jealous toward?

Scripture to Chew On

Because the patriarchs [Joseph's brothers] were jealous of Joseph, they sold him as a slave into Egypt. But God was with him.

Acts 7:9 NIV

Booster Shot For Your Satisfied Life

I have always been intrigued by the relationship between Onesiphorus and the apostle Paul. (2 Tim. 1:16–17.) He often visited Paul and encouraged him. Paul was mightily used of God. He wrote more than half of the New Testament, pioneered churches, taught the Word, preached to crowds, discipled believers, and traveled extensively on missions trips during most of his ministry. Yet the Bible mentions his friend Onesiphorus as a man who showed kindness, encouragement, and hospitality to him. Onesiphorus could have been jealous of Paul, as Saul had been of David; but instead, Onesiphorus stood by Paul even when Paul was in his trials. If you have been envious or jealous toward anyone, pray for God to increase, favor, anoint, use, open doors for, and promote that person; and choose to rejoice, celebrate, and congratulate anyone and everyone who is being used by God in any way.

Day 10

Load Up On Joy

A cheerful disposition is good for your
health; gloom and doom leave you
bone-tired.

Proverbs 17:22 MSG

For years, medical science has been studying the
effects of laughter and humor and their role in the health
of our mind and body. Humor therapy is being used
for the relief of physical or emotional pain and stress.
Laughter is known to reduce muscle tension, increase
cardio-respiratory function, and reduce stress. Recent
studies show the benefits of humor and laughter on
various immune system outcomes. At the biophysical
level, laughter moves lymph fluid around our body
simply by the convulsions we experience during the
process of laughing; so it boosts our immune system
function and helps clear out old, dead waste products
from organs and tissues.

Laughter increases the oxygenation of our body at
both the cellular and organ level. When we laugh, we
intake vast amounts of oxygen. They've discovered that

cancer cells are destroyed in the presence of oxygen and many parasites and bacteria don't survive well in the presence of oxygen. Laughing also boosts circulation and exercises abdominal muscles as well as the muscles of your face. Maybe it's the next best thing to botox? The harder you laugh, the greater the effects.

I wonder if the Lord already knew all this. No wonder He told us through Paul to rejoice always! (1 Thess. 5:16.) In fact, I want to introduce you to a side of God that we don't often consider—God laughs. Yes, that's what the Bible says: God sits in heaven and laughs. (Psalm 2:4.) What do you think He laughs about? If you're like many people, you can't even imagine a God who laughs. The only God you know is the serious, austere, stern, severe, kill-joy who's ready to bop you when you mess up.

I don't pretend to know everything about God, but I do know that God is not sad or down in the dumps. How can He be when in His presence is fullness of joy? (Ps. 16:11.) When you get around God, you can't help but laugh! How have we missed this? The Bible tells us God sings and rejoices over His kids; the angels in heaven have parties when people turn to the Lord; and while on earth Jesus was loaded with more joy than anyone else. (Zeph. 3:17; Luke 15:10.) To top it off, we're told to serve the Lord with gladness and to rejoice always. (Ps. 100:2; Phil. 4:4.) Apparently, God is into joy.

God is not overwhelmed or stressed out by all the demands, He is full of joy—and so is His Son. Jesus was anointed with gladness! He was a happy, friendly, joy-filled person, not the sad-looking "homeless" guy image you see in portraits. He laughed and radiated joy. What is He so happy about? After all, doesn't He know about deadlines? Terrorists? Wars? Natural disasters? The economy? The thing that gives the Lord joy—is us! Yes, we were the joy that enabled Jesus to endure the cross. (Heb. 12:2.) God's great joy is a real, personal, growing relationship with us.

We need the joy of the Lord; it is the hallmark of the Christian life and an attribute of the Proverbs 31 Woman: "She is clothed with strength and dignity, and she laughs without fear of the future" (v. 25 NLT). Yet too many Christians are stressed and depressed or mad and sad. If we are Christlike, we are joy-filled! So, how do we load up on joy?

• *Hang Out with God.* The psalmist tells us that in God's presence there is "fullness of joy" (Psalm 16:11). When we get close to God, His joy splashes over into our life. We always become like those we associate with, so perhaps we need to hang out with God more than ever this year.

• *Shout.* Several times the Bible says, "Shout for joy" (Ps. 32:11; 35:27; 65:13). Get the idea? When was the last time you shouted for joy? Shouted out your thanks and praise to God? I guarantee if you start shouting, you will also start laughing…and you will find the joy of the Lord to be your strength. How can we not be full of joy when we have a friendship with God Almighty? Got stress? Shout it out! Feeling overwhelmed? Shout with a voice of triumph! (Ps. 47:1.)

• *Laugh Anyway.* I talked with a gal a while back who had lost her husband about a year before. Since he died, she'd been very sad. Just recently she laughed for the first time in over a year. Her words: "It sure felt good!" I'm not making light of the death of a loved one or the grieving process, but sometimes we need to just laugh when we'd rather not. Imitate God and laugh by choice. Laugh a lot. Laugh at yourself! If it's been a while, you might be surprised at how refreshing it is to laugh.

• *Talk Right.* Tell your mouth what to do. The Bible is clear on this: If you want a happy life and good days, keep your tongue from speaking evil, and keep your lips from telling lies. Turn away from evil and do good. Work hard at living in peace with others. (Ps. 34:13–14.) Do you want a happy, satisfied life and good days? Follow the directions.

• *Thank God.* Come on—why not try it—be thankful! If you'll just start thanking Him for your life, breath, family, health, blessings—the joy will come.

Sadly, I think the reason more people aren't attracted to God is because of us Christians. We often look like we've been baptized in pickle juice, rather than radiating joy and laughter. Big question—how's your joy quotient? When was the last time you enjoyed a good howl with your husband, kids, or friends? Do they see you as a laughing, joyful person? Are you a boring, predictable, dull, dutiful mom, wife, co-worker, pal? Are you a nagging, "PMSing-menopausal," stressed out, raving maniac? Do you cry more than you laugh? God laughs. Will you?

Don't let boredom, apathy, passivity, depression, discouragement, circumstances, or the blues get you down. You have so much to celebrate and be thankful for! C'mon get happy, sista-girl—life is too short to be serious all the time! Have you had a "gut-busting" laugh lately?

Scripture to Chew On

Shout for joy to the LORD, all the earth,
burst into jubilant song with music; make
music to the LORD.

Psalm 98:4–5 NIV

Booster Shot For Your Satisfied Life

The Lord gave us a wonderful gift when He gave us music. These days, we have the option to create our own unique, personalized, customized playlists full of eclectic genres. I have several—my "Fresh Worship," "Heartfelt Worship," "Moving Songs," "Love Songs," and the "Fun and Funky" playlists—that bring such joy to my soul and spirit. How about you? What's on your playlist? Do you have your eclectic playlist full of songs with various lyrics, instruments, beats and rhythms, melodies, and words that get into your spirit, soul, and body, and put you into a worshipful, happy attitude? The Holy Spirit knows what songs will renew your mind, lift your spirit, and bring you into a place of victory, joy, praise, and freedom. Ask Him to help you to create the customized playlists you need and listen to them often.

Day 11

Satisfy Your Appetite

**Blessed are those who hunger and thirst
for righteousness, for they shall be filled.**
Matthew 5:6 NKJV

A number of years ago a friend of mine delivered her first baby, who was diagnosed with what could be called an eating disorder. Simply put, the baby wouldn't eat—it wouldn't nurse, you couldn't give it a bottle; it just had no appetite. At first, the doctors couldn't figure out why this baby wouldn't eat. Normally, all babies are born with an instinct to eat, yet this baby would not eat. Eventually, they diagnosed the baby with "failure to thrive." The food was available. The mother was ready to nurse. The doctors and nursing staff were on call to assist on a moment's notice; as soon as the baby demonstrated hunger or thirst it would be fed. Unfortunately, this baby was not hungry. The baby wouldn't eat, and when it finally did, it ate sporadically and in small amounts. As a result, the baby did not grow properly.

Thousands of Christians are suffering from the effects of a similar type of disorder I call SED or Spiritual

Eating Disorder (it is not a clinical diagnosis; I'm just using this term to help illustrate a very frustrating reality that many Christians experience). Multitudes of Christians don't have good spiritual eating habits and are suffering from the dramatic effects of spiritual eating disorders, the most prevalent one being "failure to thrive." Why is it that some people get born again, and yet they have no hunger for God? They won't eat.

Some people seem to believe they can respond to the altar call and pray the prayer of salvation just to get their eternal life fire insurance. That is, they accept the Lord as their Savior with the idea that by doing so, when they die they don't have to go to hell. Beyond this "fire insurance" type of prayer, there's no real hunger or thirst for God. They don't eat. Why is that, since God and His Word are available, standing by, ready to feed a hungry Christian? Everything God wants us to know about Him, His principles for successful living, and spiritual growth are available. The milk and the meat of His Word are being served up. Yet for some reason, people with spiritual "failure to thrive" just won't eat!

Perhaps the Psalmist understood this and that is why he declared, "Oh, taste and see that the LORD is good" (Ps. 34:8 NKJV). Hunger can be stirred up; you can get your taste buds moving. How hungry and thirsty are you? Be honest. Check out your spiritual hunger and thirst level by seeing which of these statements describe you:

- I read my Bible regularly.
  I rarely read my Bible.

- I go to church every week and feel energized.
  I go to church less than once a month and if the church service goes over one hour, I get antsy.

- I look forward to our worship time and in my heart I wish we could sing and worship longer.
  I do not enjoy the musical worship time and if we sing more than three songs, I get bored.

- I pray all the time and never have enough time to pray about everything in my heart.
  I get bored in prayer, run out of things to say, and really only pray when there is an emergency.

- I listen to Christian worship music on a regular basis.
  I listen to mostly secular, pop, or country music.

- I read Christian books and magazines to feed my heart.
  I read mostly secular books, novels, and magazines.

- I try to limit my movie and TV viewing and DVD choices to things that are congruent with my faith in God.
  I watch many movies, TV shows, and DVDs that contradict my faith in God.

- I attend a Bible study or small group for spiritual growth on a regular basis.
  I am hit or miss in my attendance of Bible study or small groups.

I think you can figure out what your answers mean. Perhaps it will help you to see your answers and make the necessary adjustments. If you are hungry for God, it will take a lot of God to satisfy your appetite. The more time you spend with the Lord in honest, heartfelt conversation and in listening to Him as you read the Bible, the hungrier and thirstier you will get. So don't go on a "God-fast," eat more and more of His reality in your life. The way to stir up hunger and thirst is to eat and drink more!

Scripture to Chew On

**As a deer gets thirsty for streams of water,
I truly am thirsty for you, my God.**
Psalm 42:1 CEV

Booster Shot For Your Satisfied Life

When you are at home or work and you find yourself hungry, you probably get up and fix yourself something to eat or you do something to satisfy your hunger. Have you ever noticed that just acknowledging your hunger doesn't satisfy your hunger? You could sit in the chair all day and say, "Boy oh boy, am I hungry. I am just starving." But if you never get up from the chair and eat something, you'll continue to be hungry. It's the same way where spiritual hunger is concerned. If you are hungry for God, you have to get up and eat by making your body read your Bible, pray, and go to church on a regular basis. Just like you eat three meals a day, your spiritual life needs regular meals. Describe some proactive steps you are going to begin taking to satisfy your hunger and thirst for God on a regular basis.

Day 12

Do Marriage God's Way

Therefore a man shall leave his father and mother and be joined to his wife, and they shall become one flesh.

Genesis 2:24 NKJV

God wants happy marriages. After all, marriage is His idea. It was the first institution He created. He blessed it. He wants it to work. He wants us to have an awesome, satisfying marriage, but everyone doesn't have a marriage made in heaven. Some are enduring a marriage that is hell on earth.

In some marriages there are women who found Christ after they were married and since their husband is not a believer, they have to deal with lots of issues. Or sometimes, the husband is on fire for the Lord and the wife acts like the wet blanket. This is not God's best for either party. Then there are others with stories of adultery, chat room affairs, and all kinds of bizarre activity. If you are the wife who's reeling from the reality of your husband's unfaithfulness, and you're not even sure you can forgive, trust again, or want it to work, you need answers and godly counsel. I encourage you to talk with your pastor or Christian counselor to get the input you need for your specific situation.

Maybe you're the one who's had an affair, cheated on your husband, and now your marriage is barely hanging on by a thread. You need help in the form of godly repentance, God's forgiveness, accountability, godly counsel and strength to make right choices if your marriage is to have any chance of survival.

Fortunately, for most of our married life, my husband and I have enjoyed a marriage made in heaven. We've had our bumps, like any marriage does, but we can honestly say that because Jesus Christ is the Lord of our individual lives and the Lord of our marriage, we've experienced God's blessings in our relationship. It hasn't been easy. We've had to make a lot of decisions to put one another first and not ourselves. We've had to communicate, work it out, and forgive. We've been mad, had words, and had pity parties. In the end, we've chosen to love and forgive and God continues to knit our hearts together. I recently told my husband that I am really looking forward to our empty-nest years because we have so much fun together. I mean it, and that is a God-thing. I know everyone doesn't have this type of story; if you're in that group, be encouraged that in time and with God's help, you can.

Marriage done the world's way is hell on earth. The selfish nature of each person cannot be overcome and eventually the "love" will be gone, anger and resentment will set in, and distance and coldness will dominate a marriage. If you want to do it God's way, He'll help you make the adjustments, love with His love, and enjoy a marriage made in heaven. That kind of marriage relationship is evident in the Proverbs 31 Woman. She did marriage God's way!

Marriage is challenging and requires God's wisdom, but thank God He's willing to help us. Wisdom is practical skill and acumen. It's the ability to apply knowledge, and as they say, knowledge is power. It's true, people—and marriages—perish for a lack of knowledge; but wisdom turns the power of that knowledge into something even more powerful. It's no wonder the Bible calls wisdom the principal thing! (Prov. 4:7.) Ecclesiastes 8:5 says that "a wise man's mind will know both when and what to do" (AMP). Oh, how we need that kind of wisdom in our marriages—and in the rest of our lives!

The amazing benefits of getting wisdom are found throughout Proverbs: victory, protection, wealth, profit, prosperity, long life, honor, peace, pleasantness, a tree of life, blessings, exaltation, influence, guidance, life, health, and more. Get the idea? We all need more wisdom and God has given us a great promise regarding our ability to get wisdom:

If any of you lacks wisdom, *he should ask God,* **Who gives generously to all without finding fault, and it will be given to him**
James 1:5 NIV

The point is you don't have to sign for the package of a dissatisfying marriage, adultery, and sensual temptations that the devil delivers to your marriage every month. Instead, ask God for wisdom. But in getting God's wisdom, know that it's still going to take work. In a perfect world, both the husband and wife are surrendered to the Lordship of Jesus Christ, both are functioning in their God-given roles and walking in love. It makes it a lot easier, but it still takes work to grow and maintain a godly marriage. It takes humility, patience, and forgiveness—and that takes a marriage of three.

God's Word clearly outlines the secret to walking in His blessings as a husband and wife—the third Person in our marriage needs to be Jesus Christ. When He is allowed to take His place in our life and marriage, His plan for a satisfying marriage goes into operation.

Scripture to Chew On

A threefold cord is not quickly broken.
Ecclesiastes 4:12 NKJV

Booster Shot For Your Satisfied Life

I want to share with you the "True Love Triangle" exercise to put things into perspective. It starts with drawing a triangle on a sheet of paper. At the top point of the triangle put the word Jesus. At the bottom left of the triangle write your name. At the bottom right of the triangle write your husband's name (fiancé's name, boyfriend's name, or if you're waiting for God's mate for you, write "to be announced").

Now, draw an arrow on the outside of the triangle that goes from your name up to Jesus. Draw an arrow on the outside of the triangle that goes from your husband's name up to Jesus.

If both individuals are focused on Jesus Christ and growing in their relationship with Him, notice what happens to the distance between the husband and the wife as each person gets closer to Jesus. Notice the distance between the husband and wife by looking at the bottom line of the triangle. Now, draw three horizontal lines inside the triangle that are parallel with the bottom line of the triangle. Each line gets smaller and smaller as you get closer to Jesus. This represents the reality that the husband and wife get closer and closer to one another as they purpose to get closer to Jesus. Thus, a threefold cord is not easily broken. This is God's best: a marriage of three.

Day 13

Be a Spout, Not a Sponge

Wives, understand and support your husbands in ways that show your support for Christ. The husband provides leadership to his wife the way Christ does to his church, not by domineering but by cherishing.

Ephesians 5:22–24 MSG

The story goes that a woman died and went to heaven. When she got to the Pearly Gates, she asked St. Peter how to get into heaven. Peter said, "It's simple, just spell one word—love."

The woman proceeded to spell L-O-V-E perfectly and Peter welcomed her into heaven. After a few moments, he asked her to guard the Pearly Gates while he ran an errand, and she asked, "What should I do if someone shows up at the Gates?"

Peter replied, "You'll know what to do." He left and within a few minutes the woman's husband showed up at the Pearly Gates.

"What are you doing here?" she asked him.

"I don't know," the man answered, "I must have died and now here I am at the Pearly Gates. How do I get in?"

"It's easy," she responded, "you just have to spell one word."

"Really?" he said, "What's the word?"

"*Czechoslovakia*" she answered! (In case you wondered, this is not how you get into heaven!)

Doesn't sound like a happy marriage, does it? I've seen this kind of attitude with married couples up close and personal. A husband or wife is in a season of frustration in their marriage and they make wrong choices on how they treat their spouse. Hollywood makes self-centeredness in marriage look normal. The problem is that in real life, it creates heartbreak and pain for all parties involved. Often, as time goes on, the ones who made selfish choices often have nothing but their material possessions to show for their lives. They've inherited nothing.

Remember, building a satisfying marriage and being the wife you are called to be begins by knowing that you are complete in Christ. (Col. 2:10 NKJV.) Some single women say, "I feel like half a person. I can't wait to meet my spouse so I will finally feel complete." That's faulty thinking. While your husband can be one of God's major blessings in life, he is not supposed to take the place of God in your life. Jesus is the satisfier of our heart and whenever we try to find our satisfaction in anyone else, we will be let down. Other people, even our husband, are not designed to fill that role for us. When Jesus satisfies you, it frees you up to be a spout of blessing, rather than a sponge that needs something from others.

God's plan for your marriage is possible when you are secure and fulfilled in your own relationship with Him *because you are able to choose to be a giver and focus on your spouse's needs rather than your own*. The Proverbs 31 Woman knows something about this role of hers and how to bring out the best in her husband and in their marriage.

> **The heart of her husband trusts in her confidently and relies on and believes in her securely, so that he has no lack of [honest] gain or need of [dishonest] spoil. She comforts, encourages, and does him only good as long as there is life within her.**
> *Proverbs 31:11,12 AMP*

Trust is a huge issue in marriage. Jealousy, anger, accusation, and suspicion stem from a heart of distrust. Cultivating trust in marriage will bring a great deal of peace and tranquility. How she relates to him is the reason her husband's heart can trust, rely, and believe in her: "she...richly satisfy his needs" (v. 11 TLB). According to many marriage experts, our husbands' needs can be boiled down to these basics.

He Needs Affirmation and Admiration. The apostle Paul made a statement similar to Proverbs 31:11–12 using twelve words that help us know how we should relate to our husbands.

> **Let the wife see that she *respects* and *reverences* her husband [that she *notices* him, *regards* him, *honors* him, *prefers* him, *venerates*, and *esteems* him; and that she *defers* to him, *praises* him, and *loves* and *admires* him exceedingly].**
>
> ***Ephesians 5:33*** AMP

You know your husband has faults—so do you. Criticizing and finding fault is the easy part. The challenging part that goes against our human nature is to focus on your spouse's strengths. Earlier in this passage in verse 22 Paul calls this "submitting yourselves unto your own husbands, as unto the Lord" (KJV).

These days *submission*[1] has become a negative word in Christian as well as secular circles, so this verse goes against our culture of male-bashing. I am all in favor of women being strong and independent, but at the same time God wants our marriages to be healthy, flowing with His structure, and blessed. Remember, that's only possible when we do things God's way.

He Needs a Fun Friend and Recreational Companion—God wants husbands and wives happy! In Ecclesiastes 9:9 TLB, King Solomon, the wisest king who ever lived, said,

> **Live happily with the woman you love through the fleeting days of life, for the wife God gives you is your best reward down here for all your earthly toil.**

If your marriage theme is based on hearing you roar (remember that old 70s song?), how about putting your "gun" down and looking for ways to enjoy life with your husband? You might be surprised to know that he'd like to spend more time with you, if you weren't whining or criticizing him.

My husband loves to ride his motorcycle with me as his passenger. We make it a point to go for rides and often find little cafés or back roads to visit and have a great time together. He wants and needs my companionship and these little trips have helped bond us together. If your husband likes to fish, or watch football, or ride bikes, why don't you ask him if he'd like your company and enjoy these recreational hobbies together? What is his favorite meal? Restaurant? Activity? Surprise him and enjoy it together and watch your bond with him grow stronger.

He Needs Sexual Fulfillment. Sex is a God thing as well as a good thing. He created us to enjoy sexual relations with our spouse. Reaching fulfillment in the sex act brings a great deal of unity, joy, and peace to the marriage relationship. Unfortunately many Christian gals have been given an unhealthy view of sex with their spouses and they "endure" or dutifully perform sex with their husbands, rather than enjoying it. We may be created differently from our husbands regarding how the passion gets going in us—wives need more emotional and physical touch whereas husbands are turned on merely by looking at our body—but God wants us to enjoy sex as much as our husbands do! Generally speaking, our husbands are going to have a stronger sex drive than us gals, but it's important that we do our best to keep up and be the one who satisfies our husband's God-given need for sexual intimacy.

Paul said it this way, "The husband should fulfill his wife's sexual needs, and the wife should fulfill her husband's needs. The wife gives authority over her body to her husband, and the husband gives authority over his body to his wife. Do not deprive each other of sexual relations… so that Satan won't be able to tempt you because of your lack of self-control" (1 Cor. 7:3–6 NLT).

Treating your husband well will enable him to be the best he can be—his confidence rises, he is satisfied with his wife and family, and he is able to fulfill God's plan for his life. Usually there are challenges along the way and it may seem that all of the "seeds" you are planting aren't producing much of a crop in your marriage or family, but if you will hold your position and continue to do good to your husband, you will see the fruit: "Her husband is greatly respected when he deliberates with the city fathers" (Prov. 31:23 MSG). In other words, he is "known, taken notice of, and celebrated...for his wisdom...and for being the husband of such a woman"[2] as you!

Scripture to Chew On

Marriage should be honored by all.
Hebrews 13:4 NIV

Booster Shot For Your Satisfied Life

God wants you and your husband to be as free with each other as Adam and Eve were in the garden before the fall. Write a 50-word "gush" describing the great traits of your husband. What do you think about sharing it with him?

Day 14

Make Your Kids Rich In God

Children are a gift from the LORD; they are a reward from him…How joyful is the man [and woman] whose quiver is full of them!

Psalm 127:3,5 NLT

I remember the day that my grandiose visions of being June Cleaver[1] flew out the window. Our oldest daughter, Meghan, was ten, and our son Luke was bothering her while she was picking at the healthy meal I'd made. (Like a good new mother, I had every good intention of feeding my children healthy, balanced meals—but then, I regained consciousness!) *"Mommmmm,"* Megan whined, "Luke just looked at me!" Wow, what a crisis, so I ran to the rescue, "Luke, tell Meghan you're sorry." He rolled his 6-year-old eyes and said, "Sorry," then burped in her face.

Children are a blessing from the Lord and He loves them more than we do—that's a good thing to remember when you've had a crazy day with preschoolers or a rough week with hormonal teenagers or a heartbreaking season with a wayward child. Raising kids is a joy and a challenge, a huge honor and responsibility.

As moms, our hearts long for nothing more than to raise kids who turn out right—kids who love God, know God, and serve God; kids who are obedient, kind and giving, joyful, articulate and confident, successful, and eventually happily married. We want to raise kids who are unselfish and servanthearted; kids who feel worthwhile and valuable. It's our goal to help them become healthy and balanced spiritually, emotionally, mentally, and physically. We all know it doesn't happen by accident.

The way God wants us to be mothers (He wants fathers to be this way too) is to train up our kids to leave home and to become independently dependent on Him. When we raise kids God's way, it's a big challenge because we are swimming against the culture—but with God's help and wisdom we can do it. (If you don't have children for whatever reason, you can use what you learn here to help other children you know. If your children are grown and you weren't a Christian when you raised them, you can still put this information into practice for them.)

Motherhood has so many dynamics—training children, disciplining, loving and nurturing, being an example, teaching the Word. But one of the most important roles mothers have is the responsibility and privilege of praying for our children. Praying earnest, heartfelt, continued prayers according to God's Word can make a difference for our kids. Our prayers will make tremendous power available for them and make supernatural deposits for their spiritual welfare. As we pray for our children, we are putting God's power on deposit for them to withdraw at the needed time. Isn't that amazing? Our prayers make our kids rich in God!

How can we pray in such a way that we know we have results? If we ask God on behalf of our children for anything according to His Word, we can know He hears us, and if we know He hears us, we know that we have the thing we have asked Him. (1 John 5:14–15.) What kind of prayers can we make?

Pray for your child to know Jesus. Start today declaring that your children (name them) fear the Lord and delight in doing His will and commands.

Pray for your child to be filled with God's Word. Our son Luke was really questioning his belief in God. He told me he wanted to see God and he didn't understand why God wouldn't just "appear" to him. We talked about it and I told him to read his Bible and see if the Lord spoke anything to his heart. A few days later, Luke told me he felt like God answered him when he read John 1:18: "No one has ever seen God. But the unique One, who is himself God, is near to the Father's heart. He has revealed God to us" (NLT). God said more to my son in one verse than I had said in twenty minutes. Luke didn't get to "see" God, but he heard from God in a personal way through the Word. Helping our kids develop this type of relationship with God and His Word will serve them for their entire lives.

Pray that your child would be led by the Spirit. First Samuel 3:1–10 is a great story on how children can hear God's voice and be led by Him. When the prophet Samuel was a young boy, he woke up one night when God called out to him; but he thought it was Eli, the high priest. When Eli realized it was God, he instructed the boy to go lie down and answer the Lord when He called him again. Samuel did, and God foretold him of things to come in Eli's life. Later, Samuel was established as a prophet and the Lord continued to reveal Himself to him and lead him.

Pray for your child to live by faith. Timothy not only got his knowledge of the Scriptures from his mother and grandmother, he got his faith and trust in God from them: "I know that you sincerely trust the Lord, for you have the faith of your mother, Eunice, and your grandmother, Lois" (2 Tim. 1:5 TLB). Living by faith pleases God and reaps His rewards. (Heb. 11:6.)

Pray for your child's personal maturity. God has wired each of our children to have a God-given temperament, spiritual gifts, and unique ways of communicating. If we try to fit our children into our cookie cutter mold of what we want them to be, we'll frustrate the grace God has given them to be the person He's created them to be. It's our responsibility to discover the way God has wired them and then cooperate with Him in nurturing those things and helping them to reach their greatest God-given potential. Proverbs 22:6 (MSG): says "Point your kids in the right direction—when they're old they won't be lost." Pray for God's wisdom and grace to point your kids in the right direction and help them choose the right path in life.

Pray for your child's education and learning. The book of Daniel tells of four young men whom "God gave" such "an unusual aptitude for learning the literature and science of the time," that the king sought their advice instead of "all the magicians and enchanters in his entire kingdom" (Dan. 1:17,20 TLB). Notice that passage says, "God gave." We can pray that they will live for God as those young men did, and we can trust Him to bless our children in their learning, as well.

Pray for your child's friends and mate. Proverbs 18:24 says that to have a friend we must be a friend. The wrong kind of friends, though, can ruin a child's good character. (1 Cor. 15:33 NIV.) You can pray for godly friends and divine, God-knit friendships for your kids. Also pray for your children to be friendly, confident, and outgoing so that they make good friends. And it's never too early to pray for God's best choice for your child's spouse. He is the One who can order their steps to one another in His timing. Most of all, pray that Jesus would be their best friend, the "friend who sticks closer than a brother" (Prov. 18:24 NKJV).

Pray for your child's sexual purity. These days our kids are truly being bombarded by sexual impurity! It's in your child's best interest to help them and pray for them to live pure lives. As moms, we mustn't set the bar too low—expect the best from you kids in purity, dating, dress, and lifestyle choices. Impart God's values to them and pray that His Word and wisdom takes root in their hearts. God wants our kids to "keep clear of all sexual sin. Then each of you will control your body and live in holiness and honor—not in lustful passion as the pagans do, in their ignorance of God and his ways" (1 Thess. 4:3–5 TLB). This is a great passage to pray when praying for your child in this area.

Pray for your child's well-being and long life. We live in a society of disrespect, but as believers we ought to raise children who respect their parents, their elders, and God-appointed authorities. Ephesians 6:1–3 (NIV) tells children to obey and honor their parents. When they do, God promises that it will "go well" with them and that they will "enjoy a long life on earth." (Proverbs 3 also has some great insights on how to pray for your child's welfare.) When praying about this, pray for the heart of your child to be submissive and obedient to you. Stand upon this promise of God's for your child and teach him or her to respect all authority, governmental, civil, spiritual, and educational leaders.

Pray for your child's destiny and future. We know from Jeremiah 29:11 that God has good plans for our children—"plans to prosper [them] and not to harm [them], plans to give [them] hope and a future" (NIV). Psalm 25:4–5 tells us that God wants to show our children His ways, teach them His paths, and guide them into His truth. You can pray that your children will seek the Lord wholeheartedly and find God and His will for their lives. Also, that God's plan, His divinely implanted sense of purpose, and His ways are fulfilled in their lives. That He opens their hearts and spiritual eyes to desire and understand His destiny and purpose for them, and that He orders their steps. Start today to pray for your children's future!

Remember, no matter what tactics the enemy tries to throw against your family, Satan is defeated and you, your spouse, and your kids belong to God. As you stand strong in your walk with the Lord, He will give you the wisdom and strength you need to keep your kids in a good place in God. Not only that, He will go to work in their hearts doing all kinds of unseen work. God wants your children to be blessed!

Scripture to Chew On

Behold, children are a heritage from the LORD, the fruit of the womb is a reward.
Psalm 127:3 NKJV

Booster Shot For Your Satisfied Life

We have to discipline, set boundaries, train our children, and pray for them; but we can be joyful mothers too. The Proverbs 31 Woman encourages us as moms: "her children rise up and call her blessed" (v. 28 AMP). What child wouldn't rise up and call their mom blessed if she's a happy mom—one who laughs easily, enjoys her children, and is full of joy? Describe some funny stories you've experienced with your kids. When was the last time you goofed off with them? Played hide and seek? Stuck a French fry up your nose? Beat them in a burping contest? Decide to have fun with your kids each day and watch your satisfaction level begin to rise!

Day 15

Improve Your Serve

For you have been called to live in freedom—not freedom to satisfy your sinful nature, but freedom to serve one another in love.

Galatians 5:13 TLB

When you think of great people, who comes to your mind? What qualities make them great in your thinking? Is it their Christianity? Their relationship with the Lord? Character? Accomplishments? Influence? Wealth? Generosity? Kindness? Wisdom? What makes a person great in God's eyes?

One day several of Jesus' disciples were discussing this very thing. They were disputing among themselves as to who was the greatest among them. (Mark 9:33–35.) They were vying for the top spot on God's list. The most interesting thing is Jesus' response. He did not rebuke them for their desire to be great. He did not scold them for such an unrighteous desire. Rather, He defined greatness. His definition: Be the servant of all.

It's a sacrifice to serve. We have to say no to our wants. We have to rearrange our schedules. We have to sacrifice and give up some things, trusting that if we do so with the right motives and for the right purpose, God will add whatever we need back into our lives. William Booth, the founder of the Salvation Army, in his final address to the army soldiers got up and simply said, "Others." With that, he sat down. Talk about making an impact!

The best place to start serving others is in our families. My husband is the most servant-hearted person I know. He serves me and our kids in the most consistent and creative ways. For instance, he is a morning person and several years ago he decided to start getting up early to make breakfast for the kids and have some dad-chat and devotion time with them before they go to school. He always seems to think ahead and he looks at the needs in our home and finds a way to serve. It's remarkable. Compared to him, I have room for improvement!

Let's look at the Proverbs 31 Woman to see how she served her family.

> **She gets up before dawn to prepare breakfast for her household and plan the day's work for her servant girls.**
>
> *Proverbs 31:15 NLT*

According to this verse, making breakfast is a way we can serve our family. Not only that, but it sounds like she gets up early! Are you an early-riser girl? What type of plan do you have for meals for your family? If you are like a lot of American families on the go, you probably find it hard to get everyone together for dinner on a regular basis. We have four children who are involved in sports and school activities, and at times it's a matrix challenge just to find a night everyone will be home to eat dinner. Eating breakfast together works better for us. Find out what works with your family's schedule and stick with that.

> **She makes for herself coverlets, cushions, and rugs of tapestry. Her clothing is of linen, pure and fine, and of purple [such as that of which the clothing of the priests and the hallowed cloths of the temple were made].**
>
> **Proverbs 31:22 AMP**

It sounds like she is a talented seamstress and a great decorator. It sounds like she gives her bedroom a makeover on occasion and makes her home comfortable and homey. In what ways could you serve your family through decorating and creating a warm environment for them? You don't have to be a talented seamstress or decorator to make your home attractive and appealing.

It's been said that "a man's home is his castle." We really do honor the Lord as we serve our family by keeping a clean, uncluttered, nicely decorated house. Have you taken a look around your home lately? Do the kids' bedrooms need a decorating update? Is your master bedroom a love nest for you and your spouse? There are so many creative ways to decorate on a shoestring budget these days, so why not set aside some time to update your décor if it needs it.

One of God's best blessings is our families. Unfortunately, this is the group that we sometimes take for granted. Worse, these are the people we often hurt the most and when we trouble our own house, it is to our detriment. In the event you have been doing that—all is not lost. If you will talk to the Lord, genuinely repent, express your heartfelt sorrow for hurting your family, and if you will go the extra 100 miles to rebuild some bridges, invest in lines of communication, and demonstrate humility and countless selfless acts of love towards your family members—your ex, spouse, kids, grandkids and other loved ones—over time (sometimes a long time) you may be able to restore what has been lost. It may not be easy and it may take time. But, with God and His mercy and grace, all things are possible.

Scripture to Chew On

Serve the LORD with gladness.
Psalm 100:2 NKJV

Booster Shot For Your Satisfied Life

The Proverbs 31 Woman "watches over the affairs of her household and does not eat the bread of idleness" (v. 27 NIV). Sleeping in until noon, watching TV all afternoon, and then serving boxed macaroni and cheese for dinner is an example of an idle woman. God wants us to be actively serving our families. We can serve our families by acting as the "air traffic controller," keeping track of all their activities, domestic needs, and affairs. Why not think about new ways to serve your own family—how you can cheer for, invest in, bless, reach out to, communicate with, encourage, build up, nurture, care, talk to, give into, and love them deeply. In what ways have you been serving your family and watching over the affairs of your household? In what ways can you improve?

Day 16

Find Your Girls: You've Gotta Have Friends

The sweet smell of incense can make you feel good, but true friendship is better still.
Proverbs 27:9 CEV

One summer, I hosted the neighborhood Bunco group and my husband just stared in amazement at the non-stop slur of girl-chitchat increasing in decibels every round. At one point, he had the audacity to ask us what the object of Bunco was. Who knows? Who cares? We played Bunco to talk! Color coordinated plates and napkins, cheese and crackers, Twizzlers and M & M's… life is good! The bell rang, we rolled the dice, someone shouted "Bunco," and the talk-a-thon was on. We didn't care whose turn it was; our concerns (talking about life stuff) were more important!

Girls and friendship…they're like peanut butter and jelly—they just go together! I can't imagine life without friends. Can you? What would going to a favorite restaurant or shopping at the mall be like without a chick friend? How do you survive a carpooling crisis without a friend? Who do you call when you need prayer? Who do you share your extra 10,000 words a day with? Without girlfriends, life would be so full of testosterone! We love our men, but boys are not girls. Girls talk; therefore we are friends.

I've met a lot of lonely women—married, single, moms, professionals—busy women, yet lonely inside. If you're feeling alone, tapped out, overloaded, or like it's you against the world—look around! God always strategically places people in our lives to help us. They aren't always easy to find, but if you'll look, they are there. When that dull, helpless feeling creeps up on you or you start to stress out by drawing from your own human ideas, knowledge, wisdom, or experience, stop going it alone. Draw on the ideas, knowledge, wisdom, and experience God has given to others.

Friends help sharpen us: "Iron sharpeneth iron; so a man sharpeneth the countenance of his friend" (Prov. 27:17). Ever felt dull? Not sharp? Worn down? Overwhelmed? Depleted? Out of fresh ideas or energy? You need friends! You need a team of people to help sharpen you.

Sometimes, we give people the impression that we are a rock or an island and we have it all together. Let's just admit, we aren't and we don't. Let people in your world know that you welcome the "sharpening" power they bring to your life. We are the body of Christ and we need each other.

In my husband's and my own experience, we cannot tell you the relief, refreshing, joy, power, fruit, and multiplied strength we have received from the various people God has put in our lives. For a lot of years, as we pioneered a church, we tried to do things "alone," but when we started developing teams, asking for and receiving the "sharpening" power of others—it was a happy day! We learned that asking for help isn't a sign of weakness; it's a sign of great strength.

Some of God's greatest blessings are people! Sometimes just talking or praying with a friend does wonders for our stress level. Be sure to appreciate and cultivate the friendships God has placed in your life and you will find relief from much of the stress and overload you may feel. Remember that there are high maintenance friends and there are those who pour blessing and refreshment into our lives. Just because someone calls themselves a friend doesn't mean they are.

Jesus said we'd know people by their fruit. Judas called himself a follower back in the day and so did John. Judas was a pious pretender. In a moment when Jesus needed him most, Judas showed his true colors and with a pretend act of affection, betrayed Jesus into the hands of thugs. John, on the other hand, was completely different from Judas. John was a true-blue friend to the core. He was Jesus' dear friend and disciple and the one Jesus entrusted with caring for His mother. John really was a true friend. He understood the core of Jesus' message—love!

The Proverbs 31 Woman reached out to others (vv. 20,26); so should we. Wherever they are—at the PTO, Junior League, church or Bible study, neighborhood coffee, cohorts at work, Bunco—I encourage you to find your girls! Take the initiative. Invite a stranger out for coffee. Make new friends, but keep the old. The point is you've got to have friends.

Yet, no matter the size of our circle of friends and family—even with a wonderful husband, children, and the dearest girlfriends—there is still going to be a place inside of us that longs for Someone to know and understand the deepest part of us. Good news...there is a Friend who sticks closer than a brother (Prov. 18:24) and I hope you get to know this Friend, too. You can know Him intimately through friendship with Him in His Word.

It's a terrible thing to feel alone. Rejected. Depressed. Trapped. Imprisoned. Hollow. Alone in the big fat universe. Lonely in a crowd. Lonely in a marriage. The irony is that is how it was designed; we were meant to be lonely. While we need other people in our lives, the plan is that no other human being, no created thing, no experience—nothing at all—can fill, fulfill, or complete us.

We live behind our own eyeballs and no one can get there—including us. We can't even eliminate loneliness by keeping company with our own addicted self. Isn't it crazy? It is! That's exactly the way God designed it. Jesus dealt with this reality when everyone forsook Him. "You will leave me all alone. Yet I am not alone, for my Father is with me" (John 16:32 NIV).

When we know the Father is with us, we are not alone. Truly. Now this is good news for the people in our lives. It means we can lower the bar. We don't expect anyone to take away our aloneness and this is quite freeing!

This reality means our lonely days are gone. Our Father is with us. If we believe that, then we are not alone, lonely, or suffering from loneliness. If you believe it, that's the key. I might have a thousand dollars in the bank, but if I don't believe it, that money isn't going to change my life one iota. I'm still feeling broke. God is with me, never leaves me, never forsakes me—if I believe it, that can change my life.

Scripture to Chew On

A man who has friends must himself be
friendly, but there is a friend who sticks
closer than a brother.

Proverbs 18:24 NKJV

Booster Shot For Your Satisfied Life

God loves to surround our lives with wonderful
people. Do you feel that you are alone? Remember that
you have God, plus all the people He has put in your
life. Today, look at your life and find those precious,
intuitive, creative, Jesus-loving people you can trust and
replenish friendships God has given you. Who's your "go
to" friend in times of crisis, need, and rejoicing? Who's
on your "sharpening" team? Who can you lean on? Call?
Float an idea by? Shoot an email to? Bounce an idea off
of? Have a cup of coffee and brainstorm with? Do it!

Day 17

"Go, and Do Likewise"

If any man serve me, let him follow me; and where I am, there shall also my servant be: if any man serve me, him will my Father honour.

John 12:26

We've become a consumer society where people expect to be served, rather than serve. Ask any church about the difficulty they have in recruiting children's ministry workers and you'll hear great excuses people use for not serving.

There is nothing more unbecoming than a self-absorbed woman. Yes, we need to serve our spouse and family, but serving isn't limited to "us four and no more." These days there are too many gals with the *me, my, and mine* mantra: *My life, my husband, my family, my money, my education, my job, my hobbies, my stuff. It's all about me!* I hope this is not your story, but in the event it is, there is only one solution to this mentality—get over yourself! Serve.

I am a big advocate of serving God and serving others. The Proverbs 31 Woman serves her family, but she also serves those in her sphere of influence. She looks for ways to help people who have all kinds of needs: "She opens her hand to the poor, yes, she reaches out her filled hands to the needy [whether in body, mind, or spirit]" (v. 20 AMP). Notice that she is led by the Lord to seek out not just the poor in material goods, but also the poor spiritually, the poor mentally, and the poor in body.

Perhaps you have some practical ways that you reach out to the "poor" in your world. God says much on this in His Word, but one particular verse stands out to me.

> **The Spirit of the LORD is upon Me, because He has anointed Me to preach the gospel to the poor; He has sent Me to heal the brokenhearted, to proclaim liberty to the captives and recovery of sight to the blind, to set at liberty those who are oppressed.**
>
> *Luke 4:18 NKJV*

Jesus declared in Luke 4:21 that He was the fulfillment of this verse. In the book of Luke, Jesus also mentioned being about His Father's business and that we should "Go, and do likewise." (Luke 2:49; 10:37.) We can individually reach out to many types of people when we are filled with God's Spirit. Most of us have at least one person in our sphere of influence who fits the verse 18 descriptions. God promises that if we are kind to them, He measures that as lending to Him and rewards us for it. (Prov. 19:17 NIV.)

One rewarding way to be busy about the Father's business is to serve in your local church. Jesus is building His Church these days and if you haven't served yet in yours, I encourage you to get busy. The power of a local church in a community is immeasurable. The gospel is preached and families are ministered to through the local church. A local church full of servant-hearted people can absolutely influence a city for Jesus Christ. The local church facilitates outreaches to the needy, to prisoners, and to the poor in such a way as not only to "provide a fish," but to "teach people how to fish" so they get lasting help. The Church is front and center for Jesus! He said He would build His Church and the gates of hell would not prevail against it. (Matt. 16:18.) I believe that every Christian ought to be serving families, the poor, and their church community in some capacity through their local church.

Usually, one of the main reasons people have an issue with being involved in a local church is lack of time. We all have the same amount of time each day, each week, and each month, and we must decide how much of our time we will sacrifice in service for God's glory.

Other reasons some people rebel against church involvement is that they have pride or control issues, or are simply ignorant about the priority Jesus places on the local church.

Jesus is the Head of the Church, and as the Great Shepherd of the sheep, He's focused on helping the undershepherds pastor the sheep in a local church while they reach out to a community to build His Church. If you are not part of a local church with a God-ordained pastor, you are out of step with Jesus, the Head of the Church. If you have personal issues with church, I really encourage you to take it to the Lord in prayer and seek His will in this matter.

I love the way the *Message Bible* describes serving in it's translation of Ephesians 4 where it talks about "skilled servant work" and "working within Christ's body, the church, until we're all moving rhythmically and easily with each other, efficient and graceful in response to God's Son, fully mature adults, fully developed within and without, fully alive like Christ" (v. 13).

When we serve others in some way, not only do we receive back a great sense of fulfillment but we become "fully alive like Christ." What could be more satisfying than that?

Scripture to Chew On

Serve the LORD with gladness.
Psalm 100:2 NKJV

Booster Shot For Your Satisfied Life

One way we can serve others is with our prayers. Epaphras was a prayer warrior and he prayed for the people in the church at Colossae to stand perfect and complete in all the will of God. The Amplified Bible makes it clear that Epaphras was a servant of the Lord. (Col. 4:12.) Describe the biblical importance of serving in and through your local church. In what capacity are you serving in your church? If you haven't done that yet, where do you feel you could get plugged in and begin to serve? Could you be an Epaphras? Do you know any people in your church or sphere of influence who need your prayers?

Day 18

Discover Your Sweet Spot

> It's in Christ that we find out who we are
> and what we are living for. Long before
> we first heard of Christ and got our hopes
> up, he had his eye on us, had designs on
> us for glorious living, part of the overall
> purpose he is working out in everything
> and everyone.
>
> *Ephesians 1:11–12 MSG*

What on earth are you here for? Women want to know their purpose! I believe The *Purpose-Driven Life* by Rick Warren has been a national best-selling book because people crave fulfillment of their purpose.[1]

When you think about it, we are each allotted the space of several decades or so to live life, fulfill our destiny, potentially raise a family, leave a legacy, reach people for Christ, and influence our world. Then, one day our "blip" will fall off the radar screen as we die and go into eternity. It's sobering, isn't it? Young girls dream about what they will become. High school and college-aged girls ask questions about their purpose and destiny. Young career women and moms begin to step into part of their destiny. Women nearing midlife begin to think seriously on the purpose, value, and influence of their lives. Those in the twilight years wonder if they fulfilled their destiny and are either quite satisfied or full of regret.

People who have not yet discovered their divine destiny, and so are not yet walking in it, are very unsatisfied, empty, and disillusioned. Yet, the most miserable people on Earth are those who have discovered their divine destiny, but are going 180 degrees in the opposite direction of fulfilling it. It's no wonder that so many celebrities, rock stars, and athletes hit rock bottom and go into rehab because they are using their God-given gifts doing things God never intended for them to do. They've missed their purpose. Thank God, He's merciful and the moment we repent and turn to Him with a sincere heart, He extends His forgiveness and grace and we can get started fulfilling His purpose for our lives.

I discovered my destiny in college. I came to Christ just before my sophomore year and started serving the Lord on Spring Break; it was my first experience of being in ministry. I was a "green" Christian and we poured ourselves into evangelism as we talked to hundreds of kids about the Lord on Daytona Beach. Only a few years earlier I had been without Christ—one of the lost partiers on that beach having a "big time" as a high school senior. Now here I was "preaching on the beach" and launching into what would become a wonderful journey of ministry. I was hooked. Nothing was more exhilarating than being able to lead someone to Jesus. Thirty years later, I still feel the same way. There's nothing like the sweet spot of God's will and walking in the calling and purpose for which He created us.

How about you? What have the past few decades looked like for you? What will the next 30 years hold? Have you launched into the wonderful world of ministry? Do you wonder if God has called you to something? Maybe you wonder what gifts and talents God has given you for a specific purpose.

To help you evaluate your God-given gifts, answer the following questions and perhaps you'll be able to see a pattern revealing your giftings and find your purpose.

Your Thoughts: We often think about the areas we are called or gifted in—those gifted in music think about music; writers think about writing, and so on. What do you spend the majority of your time thinking about?

Your Time: How do you spend your time? Your weekdays? Weekends? We usually spend time on the areas we are bent towards.

Your Abilities: It's pretty obvious that many of your gifts or callings will be easy to recognize simply because you have a unique God-given giftedness, talent, or ability in an area. Often, our friends see our gifts better than we do and if we are open, they can give us their honest appraisal.

Your Service: What types of service do you lean toward? The way you desire to serve is a good indicator of how God has wired you.

Your Relationships: How do you treat the people God has placed in your life? Are you energized or drained by people? Do you have a gift for relating to others?

Your Body: Has God gifted you with physical abilities, athletic prowess, or physical beauty? Are you using these things to serve God?

You may need a little encouragement and exhortation, so here are a few "Calling Observations" to encourage you in your pursuit of God's purpose for your life:

God delights in using imperfect people. He uses the weak to confound the wise. God uses flawed, insecure, ordinary people who will dare to believe Him to do great things. Don't wait to become perfect. Start serving God now. I don't know any perfect Christians or ministers, but I know a lot of people who have yielded their lives to Jesus—and they've received His forgiveness and empowerment to do mighty things!

Comparing ourselves with others is a recipe for defeat. We can always find people who are better at everything than we are. We need to be confident in who God has made us to be. In fact, we should take joy in not being like others. There is nothing more boring than a "carbon-copy" Christian or minister. The Lord made each one of us to be different. We have a unique flavor and gift to offer the body of Christ, so let's not compare ourselves with anyone but Jesus. Be the creative, innovative, one-of-a-kind person God has created you to be!

Love people. Kind of goes without saying, doesn't it? We don't have to "like" everyone, but we are called to "love" everyone. Love means we want God's very best for others and we're willing to do whatever we can to help them experience it. God's best starts with knowing Jesus. Love people by introducing as many people as you can to Jesus Christ during your lifetime!

God has called each of us to His kingdom for such a time as this. Once you pray, evaluate yourself, and get what you believe is God's purpose and direction for you, then stay focused and start moving. God doesn't move a parked car. He can't use a car going in ten different directions, either. Sometimes, Christians get so full of vision and dreams they try to do too many things. They never focus on their sweet spot and doing one or two things well. The result is that their ministry or usefulness is diluted. Become an expert at something and do it well!

Scripture to Chew On

GOD made everything with a place and purpose.

Proverbs 16:4 MSG

Booster Shot For Your Satisfied Life

Ever wonder why some people who are exceptionally gifted fail? What shipwrecks their faith and calling? The old saying that goes, "Your gift will only go as far as your character will take you" is true—eventually, a person's giftedness will catch up to and stop at the level of their integrity. We all have unique, God-given gifts and talents that the Lord has given us to fulfill our purpose and serve others. Once you have discovered yours, be willing to take the "long route" to developing solid Christian character so that you can maximize your gifts and reach your full potential. When we allow the Lord to work in our lives to develop Christlike character, our gifts will take us a lot farther than we can imagine.

Day 19

"Pour Out" What You Have

The LORD said to [Moses], "What is that in your hand?"

Exodus 4:2 NKJV

Years ago, I read the story of a woman who did something with a Laundromat that was dirty, scary, and packed with people. She saw an opportunity and decided to buy it. She installed new washers, dryers, a fitness area, office area, coffee and juice bar, and started a singles night on Tuesdays. The result? Great success! She took what she had and "poured" her energies into making it a one-of-a-kind Laundromat.

Once we identify what we have, we need to "pour out." What we have might seem insignificant, but if we will start to "pour out" what we have, God will touch it. In modern terms, that could mean many things. Get moving. Use it or lose it. Take a first step. Get started. Do what you know to do. Just do it! Perhaps you need to make a phone call. Write a proposal. Advertise. Quit the job you hate. Start the company you've dreamed of. Pitch your idea to a corporate bigwig. Take a risk.

I know women who have amazing talents. In many cases, those skills have a marketable value that can increase as they intentionally, strategically, and wisely "pour out" in fresh ways and allow the Lord to multiply what they have. Maybe it's a teacher who retires to become a "Family Consultant"; or a hair stylist whose people skills help launch them into some entrepreneurial sales venture.

What could God do with what you have as you "pour out"? Mrs. Fields baked a cookie. Auntie Anne twisted a pretzel. Doing something with what you have is what separates the "women from the girls"—and it maximizes your life!

The Proverbs 31 Woman does something with what she has: "She selects wool and flax and works with eager hands… She sees that her trading is profitable, and her lamp does not go out at night…She makes linen garments and sells them, and supplies the merchants with sashes" (vv. 13,18,24 NIV). She is an astute businessperson with a great work ethic. Profit is good when you're in business. Have you ever had a job or business and found that once you paid your costs to work—childcare, gas, lunch, clothing—you really weren't profitable? The Proverbs 31 Woman understands that her business skills are profitable and she is working hard. She knows what her talents and skills are and she is developing what she has.

I love the story in 2 Kings 4 of a poor widow with two sons and how God turned her into a wealthy entrepreneur. This single mom had the creditors coming to make her sons servants as payment for her debts. Ever been in a crisis and needed God's intervention? The prophet Elijah wanted to help and he simply asked, "What do you have?" At first, she said, "Poor me, I don't have anything except this little jar of oil." Elijah didn't join her pity party. He told her to borrow containers from her neighbors, then pour oil into each one. She did, sold the containers of oil, and was able to pay her debts and save her sons.

What Elijah told her to do didn't look very supernatural. In fact, it sounded like he asked her to work hard! He didn't want her sitting around moaning and groaning, but he wanted her up and using the little bit she had. By obeying God, this woman became the manufacturer, warehouse and distribution center, marketing and sales rep, and wealthy, debt-free CEO of her own oil business in one day because she was obedient and gave God the little bit she had. He took it and touched it with His power! God blessed her enough that she could easily pay her debts and get the creditors off her back, and with the money that was left over, she and her boys could live. Now that's a business God has blessed!

Perhaps you are more creative and artsy. God calls artsy people to do incredible things too! Isn't that great? The Proverbs 31 Woman was creative—she made linen garments (v. 24)—and God specifically called and anointed two creative people, Bezalel and Oholiab, to help Moses build the tabernacle from the divine blueprint God had given him: "I have filled [Bezalel] with the Spirit of God, giving him great wisdom, ability, and expertise in all kinds of crafts. He is a master craftsman... [able to create beautiful objects from] gold, silver, and bronze. He is skilled in engraving and mounting gemstones and in carving wood. He is a master at every craft! And I have personally appointed Oholiab... to be his assistant" (Ex. 31:3–6 NLT). It was their job to use the creative skill God gave them to breathe life into His plan.

I have no doubt God is still calling "Bezalels" and "Oholiabs" to further His plans! It may be that the Lord has given you a special skill or aptitude to be like Bezalel or Oholiab. Whether your gift is in the arts, business, computers, cooking, or another area, here are a few things to help you harness it and flourish.

Seek God's heart. Keep your heart centered on the Lord. Seek first His kingdom and He will give you all the things you need to succeed in your business, creativity, or other type of calling.

Stay humble. Sometimes because you are so passionate and focused in your gifting, you may see things differently than someone else and get frustrated with people who don't see things that way. In fact, you can get bugged by those who lean toward a different gift or calling. If you aren't careful, you can even get puffed up with pride and resent the skills and abilities of other people sent to help you flourish.

Serve a "Moses." It may be that God has gifted you to help a "Moses" fulfill a God-given vision. God gives the "Moses-types" the ability to see both sides of the coin, the creative side as well as the administrative side—and everything in between. They are gifted to lead from a spiritual platform, and through a strategic blueprint and game plan, they mobilize people to accomplish God's purposes. A good "Moses" will bring all the people anointed for that purpose together to fulfill a God-ordained vision.

Jesus had a God-ordained vision of feeding 5,000 people with five loaves of bread and two fish. Initially the disciples were faced with the task and Jesus asked the disciples, "How many loaves do you have?" (Mark 6:38 NKJV). He didn't say, "Wow, there sure are a lot of people here; how in the world are we going to feed them? We just don't have enough, do we?" No, Jesus simply asked, "What do you have?" He's still asking that question. What do you have that you are willing to put into His hands? Your little bit in God's hands will be the base material for His miraculous purpose to be fulfilled.

Whatever God has anointed you with, be encouraged. Seek after His heart, stay humble, and serve a "Moses" (if God leads you there). Then watch God multiply your gifts for His eternal purposes!

Scripture to Chew On

> There is a lad here who has five barley loaves and two small fish, but what are they among so many?…Jesus took the loaves…distributed them…and likewise the fish.
>
> *John 6:9,11 NKJV*

Booster Shot For Your Satisfied Life

When my sister's oldest daughter got married and her second daughter graduated from high school, she hit a major life-season change and asked, "What do I have?" She's very creative and willing to take a risk; so she designed a very cool gift card box for her daughters' wedding and graduation receptions. It didn't seem significant, but everyone loved the box and wanted to borrow it. It was a light bulb moment for my sister—this is what she had! Soon she was talking to a manufacturer, writing her own patent, selling boxes at bridal shows, creating kellymariecollections.com, and importing her new product. She's got a new lease on life.

God never asks us to use what we don't have—He always and only uses what we have. While He wants to use all of us, He needs us to take some steps of faith; then He shows up to bless, maximize, expand, multiply, and use the little bit we give Him. What do you have? Identify those "light bulb" moments. If you allow God to touch what you have, supernatural things can happen in your life now and beyond!

Day 20

Get Grace For the Pace

Let us therefore come boldly unto the throne of grace, that we may obtain mercy, and find grace to help in time of need.
Hebrews 4:16

A few years ago my husband, Jeff, ran the Chicago Marathon. I was so proud of him. One thing the runners did was pace themselves. When the gun goes off everyone starts with a rush of adrenaline and energy, but they realize that they cannot keep a starting pace for the entire 26 miles, so they look for their stride that will allow them to finish the race.

As my husband expended more and more energy during the race, he needed replenishment. He needed glucose and water to continually energize and hydrate his body so that he wouldn't wear out before the finish line. It would have been crazy for him to presume to run the race at his pace without some type of relief along the way. Similarly, we need God's grace to help us keep the pace and finish our race!

As I stood in the grandstands that day watching everyone cross the finish line of the Chicago Marathon, I had a God moment. I thought, *Lord, this is what You see every day. People finish their race on Earth and they cross that heavenly finish line.* Some of those in the Chicago Marathon finished the race strong, energized, and full of joy. Others finished the way a lot of believers do.

The apostle Paul said that we're to "run with patience [or perseverance[1]] the race that is set before us" (Heb. 12:1). Yet many people finish their race with a limp or a stagger and others crawl across the finish line because without God, we can't finish any other way. With God, we can finish strong.

Imagine a marathon runner trying to race wearing a ski jacket, hiking boots, and motorcycle helmet. It would be too big of a burden, and just the weight of the extra clothing would wear the runner out. Often in life, we are like that runner. As we run our race, we carry the weight of the world, worries, cares, and burdens, which weigh us down. We need to unload. We need to cast our cares and get some relief. We need to upload our concerns to the Lord and receive His grace.

Grace has been defined as "Favor—strength, help, counsel, direction, support, for the various duties and trials of life."[2] God's grace is a tangible deposit; one dimension of it is an internal infusion of His strength. When we access His grace by faith, He helps us stand strong and we are supernaturally endued with His power and ability. He downloads His strength into our very spirit, our inner man, especially when we are weak. He supernaturally enables us to do what we thought we could not do; He increases our margin. He gives us His ability and helps us do what seemed humanly impossible. God's grace is a wonderful thing. The best news is that God wants to give us more and more grace!

As a woman who fears the Lord, the Proverbs 31 Woman surely receives the grace of God daily in her life. (v. 30.) I have found that the longer I walk with the Lord, the more I realize my daily need for the relief of God's grace—by which I stand. I'll bet you've discovered this, too. Like you, my husband and I live a very busy life that seems to be on-the-go more than we'd like at times. We face legitimate demands on our time and our emotional, mental, physical and spiritual quotient. Life is just plain busy and a lot of it is legitimate. We all experience seasons when it feels like there are too many needs, too much on our plate or too much to do. Right? So, what do we do?

We have two options: *Option A*: Have a Major Meltdown; *Option B*: Get Grace for the Pace.

Sometimes Option A doesn't sound too bad. Sure, the thought of having a meltdown hissy fit or a cry-a-thon sounds good on certain days. But, who wants to live like that? There is a better way. Let's just run to the throne of grace and load up!

You may be facing challenges right now such as unexpected demands, a to-do list that won't quit, overwhelming responsibilities, the straw-that-wants-to-break-the-camel's-back, spiritual battles, constant output, burdens, cares, and deadlines that make your load feel heavy. I encourage you to take time to appropriate this verse: "Be strong (strengthened inwardly) in the grace (spiritual blessing) that is [to be found only] in Christ Jesus" (2 Tim. 2:1 AMP). Be strengthened inwardly by God's grace—access His "grace for the pace." He wants you to finish your race of faith with joy. We all need His grace to keep us strengthened and replenished for an entire lifetime. His grace brings us the relief we need in our race.

Don't quit too soon…stay strong to the end. Fight the fight of faith. Run the race to the end. The Lord wants to give you a supernatural burst of "adrenalized energy"—a deposit of great grace—so you can finish strong and hit the finish line tape with joy!

Scripture to Chew On

"Are you tired? Worn out? Burned out…?
Come to me. Get away with me and you'll
recover your life. I'll show you how to
take a real rest. Walk with me and work
with me—watch how I do it. *Learn the
unforced rhythms of grace.* I won't lay
anything heavy or ill-fitting on you. Keep
company with me and you'll learn to live
freely and lightly.

Matthew 11:28–30 MSG

Booster Shot For Your Satisfied Life

If you are used to operating in God's grace, then it is
usually easy to discern when you are operating outside
of His grace. The symptoms of operating outside of
God's grace commonly include: unusual frustration,
dissatisfaction, things just not working, physical symptoms in our bodies, emotional unrest, and as someone
once put it, "It feels like taking a shower with your socks
on!" Things just don't flow. Everything seems difficult.
Does this describe any facet of your life? What can you
do to change it? Remember, God always dispenses grace
to those who come and get it.

Day 21

Say Good-bye to
"Superwoman"

It's a matter of striking a balance.
2 Corinthians 8:13 GW

Are you doing many things that you aren't even called or graced to do? In the New Testament culture, women were primarily stay-at-home wives and mothers. Today, a lot of women choose to work or they must work outside the home and they face challenges with balancing their home life, family life, and work life. As a result, women are often stressed in the pace of life because we are putting more pressure on ourselves than God Himself puts on us. How do you spin all the plates? How do you juggle every ball thrown at you? Is it possible to keep up with the Joneses? Be Supermom? Find balance? How does a girl do it all? The sad reality is that a lot of women aren't able to do it all.

Paul talked about "sticking to the limits of what God has set for us" (2 Cor. 10:13 MSG), yet often we live beyond our limitations and are out of balance in one way or another. Is it really possible to find balance in life, marriage, parenting, and work? The Proverbs 31 Woman did this and so can we.

The Proverbs 31 Woman is balanced. She's real. She has a great personality. She laughs, she's a "get 'er done" type of girl, she has street smarts, she adores her family, she has a sweet spirit, she's very influential and she loves God. She's an inspiration. What we don't see in her is some "he-woman" who wears the pants in the family. We don't see a mousy, doormat, hyper-submissive woman who's afraid of her own shadow. We don't see a stuffy, churchy, religious persona; and yet, we don't see a carnal, sleazy, flesh-dominated, addictive, sensual woman either. She's godly and she's balanced. This is what God wants for us. He's not looking for Christian clones or carbon-copy church chicks. He's looking for women like the Proverbs 31 Woman who are surrendered to Him in every way and will allow Him to emboss His thumbprint in their lives and very personalities.

Real faith recognizes God-ordained boundaries, which are where God's giftings, graces, and callings start and stop. Yet sometimes we are our own worst enemy. We don't know how to set boundaries—we don't say no. We create our own stress by not recognizing our God-given limitations.

How do we set boundaries? Here are a few verses in Proverbs 31 that uncover some important personality traits of a boundary-setting, balanced woman.

Spiritual Strength. "She girds herself with strength [spiritual, mental, and physical fitness for her God-given task] and makes her arms strong and firm" (v. 17 AMP). There's no way that we could be like the Proverbs 31 Woman without spiritual strength, the result of a strong walk with God. This woman was "on purpose" about it. She "girds" herself, which simply means to "put on like a belt."[1] She expected and actively put on spiritual strength, which led to mental strength and physical fitness. Verse 29 describes her as consistently strong in character and goodness (honesty, faithfulness, generosity, ethics, and so on). That requires a strong connection with God—a real relationship that is cultivated on a regular basis.

Led by the Spirit. "She rises while it is yet night and gets [spiritual] food for her household and assigns her maids their tasks" (v. 15 AMP). It sounds like she got "spiritual food" for her household by having her own personal quiet time with God for prayer, fellowship, and hearing from Him on behalf of her family and her responsibilities. Nowadays, we've got to know how to hear from God and be led by the Spirit and be in the right place at the right time, making the right choices and hooking up with the right people. We can't do this on our own; we need to have a daily quiet time with God where we can get spiritual food, direction, and assignments for the day. It's a great comfort to know that we don't have to be a woman, wife, or mom all by ourselves. The Holy Spirit lives inside of us and He promises to lead us when we purpose in our hearts that we will be sensitive and listen to His direction—and if we are led by the Spirit, He'll lead us into God's best! (See John 16:13.)

Organized Manager. "She brings her household's food from a far [country]...She rises while it is yet night and gets [spiritual] food for her household and assigns her maids their tasks" (Prov. 31:14–15 AMP). "She's skilled in the crafts of home and hearth, diligent in homemaking" (v. 19 MSG). Verses 15 and 19 show that the Proverbs 31 woman has organizational skills. She manages her home, her family's lives, and her own life enough to know that things are organized, prepared, and ready. Whether single or married, you know how quickly things can become chaotic at home. Organization may not be your strength, but all of us can and should manage and administrate our home. When possible, things like shopping, cleaning, cooking, laundry, and basic chores can be scheduled, assigned, and maintained on a regular basis. And think categorically!

Make little piles—a pile of appointments here, a stack of phone calls there, a bunch of errands over there. Before long, you'll feel like you're making progress in organizing your life and time.

Mentally Sharp. "She girds herself with strength [spiritual, mental, and physical fitness for her God-given task] and makes her arms strong and firm" (v. 17 AMP). What do you do to stay mentally sharp, educated, and informed? Have you considered furthering your education? Learning computer skills? Taking a college course or community education class to expand your knowledge base? We should never stop learning and growing. Even such simple things as crossword puzzles, chess, and computer games that stimulate our thinking processes are good mental exercises. Stay sharp mentally. You can do it!

Physically Fit. Verse 17 also mentions that the Proverbs 31 Woman stays physically fit. Being physically fit is important for women of all ages. Proper weight, healthy blood pressure, strong bones, and muscle mass will keep you strong and fit for serving God and enjoying life. Lots of women are plagued by weight problems and the health challenges they cause. If you are one of them, I encourage you to seek the help and support you need to lose the weight you'd like to shed. Don't squander what God paid such a high price for—God owns all of us, the physical part as well as the spiritual part, "So let people see God in and through your body" (1 Cor. 6:20 MSG). This is challenging, but Jesus purchased us and our bodies with His blood and the Holy Spirit lives inside our bodies, so let's give Him a home that reflects God's glory.

Productive and Fruitful. "Give her of the fruit of her hands, and let her own works praise her in the gates [of the city]!" (Prov. 31:31 AMP). God has established the law of sowing and reaping, a law that works, regardless of the seeds we plant. If you spend your life planting good seeds into the lives of others, you will reap a rich harvest. If you plant bad, negative, hurtful seeds into the lives of others, you will reap heartache and pain. If you choose not to plant, or through apathy and laziness you don't plant any seeds at all, you will likely reap a famine. We can see that this woman reaped the fruit of her hands—in her family, business, and influence in the city. A balanced harvest from a balanced life.

You can find balance and survive the busy pace of life—and when all else fails…there's Calgon!

Scripture to Chew On

To every thing there is a season, and a time
to every purpose under the heaven.
Ecclesiastes 3:1–8

Booster Shot For Your Satisfied Life

When we try to do more than God has called and
graced us to do, we are being disobedient and run
the risk of getting out of balance and into stress and a
sense of overload and burnout. Some women may fit
the "Superwoman" category and seemingly "do it all,"
but what has God called you to focus on? How can you
stay within your sphere and limitations? Look over the
personality traits of the balanced woman and describe
what two you most need to improve. Overall, how would
you describe the profile of the type of Christian woman
you want to be?

Endnotes

Introduction

[1] Brown, Driver, Briggs and Gesenius, "Hebrew Lexicon entry for Ravah," available from http://www.biblestudytools.net/Lexicons/Hebrew/heb.cgi?number=7301&version=kjv.

Day 2

[1] Jesus is the One "who pleads our cause; who aids and assists us; who presents our interests before the mercy-seat in the heavens. For this purpose he ascended to heaven." Albert Barnes, Barnes' Notes on the New Testament, "Commentary on Romans 8," available from http://www.studylight.org/com/bnn/view.cgi?book=ro&chapter=008, Romans 8:34.

Day 4

[1] "Or 'the doctrine of grace is in her tongue'...; the Gospel, which is called the Gospel of the grace of God, and the grace of God itself." John Gill, The New John Gill Exposition of the Entire Bible, "Commentary on Proverbs 31:26," available from http://www.searchgodsword.org/com/geb/view.cgi?book=pr&chapter=031&verse=026.

Day 7

[1] Based on information from John Gill, "Commentary on Proverbs 31:22," available from http://www.searchgodsword.org/com/geb/view.cgi?book=pr&chapter=031&verse=022.

[2] Albert Barnes, "Commentary on Galatians 3," available from http://www.studylight.org/com/bnn/view.cgi?book=ga&chapter=003, S.V. "Verse 27," Galatians 3:27.

³ Albert Barnes, "Commentary on Romans 13," available from http://www.studylight.org/com/bnn/view.cgi?book=ro&chapter=013, S.V. "Verse 14," Romans 13:14.

Day 13

¹ Submitting to your husband doesn't mean submitting to physical or emotional abuse. If you are being abused, get out of the house right now and seek help immediately from your pastor, a Christian counselor, or other reputable women's abuse organization.

² John Gill, "Commentary on Proverbs 31:23," available from http://www.searchgodsword.org/com/geb/view.cgi?book=pr&chapter=031&verse=023.

Day 14

¹ Fictional mother character in the TV show Leave It to Beaver.

² Barton W. Johnson, The People's New Testament, "Commentary on Matthew 19," available from http://www.studylight.org/com/pnt/view.cgi?book=mt&chapter=019, S.V. "14. Suffer little children."

Day 18

¹ Rick Warren, The Purpose-Driven Life, (Grand Rapids, Michigan: Zondervan), 2007.

Day 20

¹ Albert Barnes, "Commentary on Hebrews 12," available from http://www.studylight.org/com/bnn/view.cgi?book=heb&chapter=012, S.V. "And let us run with patience the race that is set before us," Hebrews 12:1.

[2] Albert Barnes, "Commentary on Hebrews 4," available from http://www.studylight.org/com/bnn/view.cgi?book=heb&chapter=004, S.V. "and find grace," Hebrews 4:16.

Day 21

[1] Brown, Driver, Briggs and Gesenius, "Hebrew Lexicon entry for Chagar," available from http://www.biblestudytools.net/Lexicons/Hebrew/heb.cgi?number=2296&version=kjv, S.V. "girds," Proverbs 31:17.

Prayer of Salvation

God loves you--no matter who you are, no matter what your past. God loves you so much that He gave His one and only begotten Son for you. The Bible tells us "whoever believes in him shall not perish but have eternal life" (John 3:16 NIV). Jesus laid down His life and rose again so that we could spend eternity with Him in heaven and experience His absolute best on earth. If you would like to receive Jesus into your life, say the following prayer out loud and mean it from your heart.

Heavenly Father, I come to You admitting that I am a sinner. Right now, I choose to turn away from sin, and I ask You to cleanse me of all unrighteousness. I believe that Your Son, Jesus, died on the cross to take away my sins. I also believe that He rose again from the dead so that I might be forgiven of my sins and made righteous through faith in Him. I call upon the name of Jesus Christ to be the Savior and Lord of my life. Jesus, I choose to follow You and ask that You fill me with the power of the Holy Spirit. I declare that right now I am a child of God. I am free from sin and full of the righteousness of God. I am saved in Jesus' name. Amen.

If you prayed this prayer to receive Jesus Christ as your Savior for the first time, please contact us on the web at **www.harrisonhouse.com** to receive a free book. Or you may write to us at:

Harrison House
P.O. Box 35035
Tulsa, Oklahoma 74153

About the Author

Beth Jones, Bible teacher, author, wife, and mother of four children, ministers the Word in a relevant and inspiring way by sharing down-to-earth insights. Beth has authored over 14 books including the popular *Getting A Grip On The Basics* Bible study series; the *Bite Sized Bible Studies* series and *The Question* series of minibooks. She also writes a free, daily e-devo, "Jump Start", for thousands of subscribers. She and her husband, Jeff, serve as the Senior Pastors of Valley Family Church, a growing congregation in Southwest Michigan. Please visit www.bethjones.org or www.valleyfamilychurch.org for more information.

Beth may be contacted at
www.bethjones.org
or at
Valley Family Church
995 Romence Road
Portage, MI 49024
269-324-5599
www.valleyfamilychurch.org

Please include your prayer requests
and comments when you write.

Other Books in the 21 Day Series

21 Days to Discover Who You Are in Jesus

By Connie Witter

Discover who you really are in just 21 days. Because of Jesus, your identity changes to be like Christ—forgiven, healed, accepted, loved, favored, and blessed. By understanding Christ's amazing sacrifice, you will develop a confidence to fulfill your destiny.

Bible teacher and author, Connie Witter shares powerful personal stories and the importance of trusting in who God says you are and His love for you, even when you feel unworthy and defeated. These short devotions will inspire you to pursue God and develop the qualities He has instilled in you for such a time as this.

Relax in God's love for you and enjoy His blessings!

978-1-57794-964-0

*Available from bookstores everywhere
or from www.harrisonhouse.com.*

Other Books in the 21 Day Series

21 Days to Your Spiritual Makeover

By Taffi Dollar

With today's busy lifestyles and a world full of distractions, it's easy to lose focus on the One who gave you life to start with. But as you begin to renew your spiritual walk, you will discover the missing peace and joy that brings order to the rest of your day.

Taffi Dollar, popular television co-host, beloved pastor, and esteemed author, helps bring clarity to what is really important in a world of urgent requests. You will see clearly how the beauty of a balanced life brings a calm and joyful attitude to living. Start your spiritual makeover today and begin a beautiful life.

978-1-57794-911-4

Available from bookstores everywhere
or from www.harrisonhouse.com.